Discovering Mid-Wales

Discovering Mid-Wales

by Don Gardner

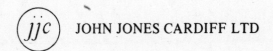

JOHN JONES CARDIFF LTD

DISCOVERING MID WALES by Don Gardner
copyright Don Gardner, 1978

First published, March 1978

ISBN 0 902375 22 9
Photographs by John Idris Jones
Jacket design by Design Types, Cardiff
Printed by Gomer Press, Llandyssul

JOHN JONES CARDIFF LTD
41 Lochaber Street
Cardiff CF2 3LS

COLOUR PHOTOGRAPHS

CONTENTS

CHAPTER ONE

THE HISTORIC CEIRIOG VALLEY

Of all the deep valleys that lead to the embattled heart of Wales, the valley of the Ceiriog retains intact today the great castle that was the bastion of English conquest of the mountain fortress of the Cymru. It stands foursquare with its great towers, overlooking the entrance to the valley road of English penetration of Wales. It is the castle of Chirk.

It was here in the valley overlooked by the castle that the mounted knights of Henry II faced the Welshmen of Owain Gwynedd in the bloody battle of Crogen. Henry had sent his woodcutters to fell the trees that were an obstacle to the advance of his armoured knights, but, in spite of this precaution, his army barely held its own. Indeed the fierce attack of the Welshmen had reached the royal standard and were threatening the life of the king himself when a brave Norman knight fought his way to the rescue and saved the king. The Dyke of Offa was filled with the corpses of both English and Welsh. Discreetly, Owain withdrew his army to fight another day.

Chirk castle today is open to the public by the courtesy of the Myddleton family who have lived there since the Civil War. The castle was first built in 1310 but, having bought it in 1595 the Myddletons did away with many draughty stone passages and windowless rooms and installed Tudor comfort. The grandeur of the state rooms and the mod cons of the domestic offices point to gracious living but the servants' quarters are spartanly Victorian with heavy oak tables and benches for seats. Strict rules of conduct for the servants, written in Victorian copperplate set out indictable offences such as cursing and swearing, telling tales and 'breeding quarrels'. The Major Domo who sat at the head of the table had the power to dock the beer allowance for the first offence and report the offender to Mr. Myddleton for the third.

No angry Welshman face you as you drive up this sequestered valley today but the limpid stream of the Ceiriog accompanies you every mile of the way.

Glyn Ceiriog

After six miles along this peaceful valley, its narrow confines broaden out to a wide amphitheatre in which stands the big village of Llanfihangel Glyn Ceiriog. Here, in the last century and the early days of this, men worked in the slate and granite quarries that surround the enclave.

Today the scars of the quarries are hidden behind a merciful screen of trees but, in their heyday they gave employment to the men of Glyn Ceiriog. Such was the output of stone and slate that a horse-drawn tramway was built to carry the stone to the boats of the Shropshire Union canal. As steam engines replaced horsepower, the trucks of the little railway were pulled by a steam engine and coaches were introduced for passengers. This was in 1885 but the railway continued working until well into the present century, taking the ladies of Glyn Ceiriog to do their shopping in Chirk and Oswestry and bringing up the coal and household goods needed in the village.

The village is now a village of bygones but it holds the finest village institute I have ever seen. This is the Ceiriog Memorial Insititute built in the honoured memory of John (Ceiriog) Hughes, a local poet of great distinction who was born at Llanarmon at the upper end of the valley. This is no ordinary village institute but a village institute of character: a memorial institute, not only to locally famous men but to famous Welshmen wherever they were born. A beautiful stained glass window carries the famous John Ceiriog as its centrepiece but one of the side panels remembers Huw Morus, the poet of Cromwellian times whose verse lambasted Cromwell and all his works. A great poet-preacher occupies the opposite panel. He was Robert Ellis of 1812-1875.

The walls and shelves of this remarkable institute are adorned with pictures and busts of great Welshmen amongst whom we find eminent doctors, statesmen like Sir David Lloyd George, and local gentry like Sir Watkin Williams Wynn. There is a billiards room, a library and a reading room. Many a sizeable town is less completely equipped with literary and recreational facilities than this country village.

I have mentioned the Civil War poet, Huw Morus, who is pictured in the stained glass window. Now we will follow George Borrow as, with his guide John Jones, he travelled up this valley, anxious to pay his tribute to this remarkable poet of the 17th Century.

The first place we reach is Pandy, with its now derelict woollen mill where the boisterous Tawr stream roars down to join the Ceiriog. (Tawr equals 'bull'. In spate it roars like a bull). Just before reaching Pandy, an enormous crag rises on the opposite side of the river. Here was the granite quarry served by the valley railway.

Here, at Pandy, we meet Borrow and walk in his footsteps.

Travelling that way a year or two ago, I came to a whitewashed cottage beside the road. Here I saw a farmer walking across the road and I asked him if Huw Morus's cottage was near. 'This is the cottage', he replied. 'This is where he lived'. The man told me his name was Joseph Bather and that the name of the cottage today was Gwercerrig, (stony farm). We talked and he told me he had lost two sons in the last war. Then he said, 'Would you like to see the chair where Huw Morus used to sit?' 'Yes, indeed I would', I replied, so he led me into the garden of the cottage. There, beside the garden path was a sort of alcove with a seat of stone and arms of stone. 'Sit in it', he said, 'Everybody does.' I duly sat but did not kiss the stone seat as Borrow did.

I thanked the obliging Joseph and went on my way. Presently I came across another cottage and here, in the garden was a monument to the famous Huw. Was this Pontymeibior where Huw lived most of his life? Did both cottages compete for the honour! I left the question unanswered.

At the end of the valley is the old village of Llanarmon where John (Ceiriog) Hughes, the nineteenth century poet of the institute was born. Here the Ceiriog river descends from its source in the Berwyns and Wayfarer, the 'rough stuff' exponent of the Cyclists Touring Club is remembered in a memorial of stone. He pioneered the route across the Berwyns followed in later years by 'Rough Stuff' C.T.C. members. We wrote our names in the Visitors' Book.

CHAPTER TWO

ROUND ABOUT Llanrhaiadr ym Mochnant - The high waterfall.

The country round Llanrhaiadr ym Mochnant shares the lonely charm of the Berwyn mountains with the rolling hills of the English Border, partaking of the beauty of both. The village itself is ancient but small and of no particular note except as a take-off for the highest waterfall in Wales. Like Nant y moch near Aberystwyth, it gets its name from pigs, ('Moch' - Pig).

The pride of the village is its history; for here, in the 16th century, the vicar was William Morgan, who through the medium of Bible Study, taught the Welsh nation how to read and write in Welsh. This he did by translating the Bible into Welsh. Previous to this historic achievement, church services were conducted in unintelligible Latin or equally unintelligible English. Now the common people could hear the Word of God spoken in their native language. A Bible became a prized possession and liable to be stolen. In churches it was chained to a reading stand or to a pillar. Even so, it was another hundred years before new techniques of printing enabled bibles to be sold cheaply enough for the poorer people to be able to afford them. It was in 1800 that Mary Jones, aged sixteen, walked twenty miles barefoot across the mountains to Bala to buy a new Bible from Dr. Charles.

LLANFYLLIN

Llanfyllin is the nearest small town to Llanrhaeadr. Its most interesting feature is its red brick church which replaced an ancient church of Welsh slate-stone. It is an anachronism to see a church in Wales built of brick like English churches, so, to atone for this un-Welshness, they gave it the sweetest peal of bells in the neighbourhood. More in character with Wales is the Wynnstay Arms hotel which is worth visiting, not only to sample the brew but to see its fine old staircase. The brew established a doubtful reputation for the beer of the town: 'Old ale fills Llanfyllin with young widows'. Perhaps this is a libel, or it may be an advertisement according to the way you look at it. In any case it refutes the charge that modern beer is 'All arms and legs' (i.e. has no body).

THE TANAT VALLEY

In the days of hectic railway building, they built a railway up the Tanant valley to take away the slate from the Llangynog slate quarries.

It was an ambitious project that would reach the Irish Sea at Porthmadog and give a through route to Ireland. Unfortunately the planners reckoned without the Berwyns which would have to be pierced with a very long tunnel to reach Bala. The idea died a natural death.

THE SAINT OF HARES

Up a secluded valley near Llangynog stands the wonderful old church of Pennant Melangell. King Brochwel, lord of the region in the year 604, was a keen hunter, and one day his greyhounds started a hare which, closely pursued, took refuge among the garments of a lovely girl kneeling at prayer. The greyhounds were nonplussed and howled their frustration. The King therefore approached and asked the girl who she was. The maiden replied that she was Monacella, daughter of King Monacella of Ireland and that she had fled her father's court rather than marry the man he had found for her. King Brochwel was so impressed with her beauty and resolution that he gave her the land adjoining her cell and built a sanctuary in which she could meditate and worship. The sanctuary became a church which rose on the site. Here she established a nunnery and lived there in peace for 37 years. In thankfulness for the happy outcome of her experience with the hare, she prayed to the Almighty that He might give her power over hares. Her prayer was granted and all the hares of the district became tame like lambs and were her constant companions.

Two effigies in stone lie in the church just inside the door. One is of the virgin saint herself and the other, incongruously, of a prince. In the year 1680, the parish register records, 'St Monacella and her thousand angels shall triumph over the powers of Hell!'

THE FAMOUS WATERFALL

At the end of the village of Llanrhaiadr a narrow road goes off unobtrusively marked 'Waterfall'. This is four miles distant but long before you reach the fall its silken skein is seen descending a great high cliff. Approaching nearer, the valley closes in to a magnificent ampitheatre of rock whose sides are clothed in lush verdure. Great pines and firs rise from the floor and sides of this spectacular cirque and at the end a cliff rises sheer to a height of over a hundred feet. Into its chasm below, and broken into a million fragments by its fall, descends a sheet of white water into a deep pool half-hidden by the mist of the spray. From this pool the stream escapes or rather spouts through a narrow tunnel of rock to fall another forty feet to the bottom pool. 'I have never seen water falling so gracefully', said George Borrow.

A close view of the main fall is obtained by crossing the wooden bridge, climbing the steep path among the trees and making the final rock traverse till one is looking down into the cauldron, (but great care should be taken on sloping rocks slippery with spray).

Borrow made friends with the occupants of the house below the falls and a woman took him along the path I have just described. From the tiny platform of rock from which one looks into the cauldron or pool a view of the escape tunnel is obtained. The woman told Borrow that she had seen a visitor, (a Russian), climb to the top of the tunnel 'like a llysowen' (eel).

Like all Welsh waterfalls, Pistyll Rhaiadr should be visited in normal rainy weather. After a long drought, the volume of water is insignificant and the fall unspectacular.

CHAPTER THREE

LAKE VYRNWY

Wales, where the blight of industry has not marred its loveliness, is a land of natural beauty. Its mountains, its rivers, its cascades and its lakes are its seductive charms and when man is in sympathy with Nature as in Vyrnwy, nature conspires to assist him. The skills and techniques of modern engineering can adapt nature to the service of man but can rarely conceal the wounds of the process. But in Vyrnwy, this remarkable result has been achieved. A 'bare and featureless valley' has been transformed into a lake whose beauty equals, if not surpasses, the charms of Nature's own handiwork.

Thirsty, affluent Liverpool was looking in 1881 for water to supplement its inadequate supplies from small local reservoirs and the great city came to Wales to find it. The broad shallow valley of the Afon Vyrnwy provided the answer. Often we find that today's dams are structures in stark concrete, functional but with no claims to architectural beauty. They reflect only the materialistic spirit of the age. The dam that Liverpool constructed was of blocks of natural stone whose masonry vies in architectural beauty with that of of Mediaeval abbeys and cathedrals. Their builders built to the glory of God as well as to the service of mankind. The gothic valve tower that releases the water to the 70-mile long pipeline has its counterparts in the castles along the Rhine.

As the new lake filled, its shores were planted with trees, with true Victorian economy. These trees of oak, pine and fir are mature today and supply valuable timber to reward the foresight of those who dreamed the enterprise of a hundred years ago.

Liverpool was justly proud of its achievement and made public its story in letter of bronze for all to read. Civic pride in achievement is seen here in the three bronze plaques artistically attached to the smoothed face of the virgin rock opposite the dam. It is good to see the public vision of city fathers and the brains and intelligence of engineers and architects thus publicly recognized.

The lake is five miles long and nearly a mile wide, filling the valley and drowning a village.

To re-house the villagers, Liverpool built the model village of Llanwddyn just below the dam: the best and only thing the city could do for the displaced people.

Today, like Birmingham's reservoirs in the Elan Valley, the lake is a mecca for visiting tourists who are able to drive right round it by a good road. A succession of little bays and inlets indents its shores giving tourists access to its waters for fishing or boating. At intervals, there are parking places for picnics and recreation. Little rivulets come down from the surrounding hills to feed the waters and in one place a deep valley brings down a powerful stream from the pass of Swlch y groes to join the lake. The circuit of the lake is a ten-mile drive.

At the far end of the lake is the road to Bala. This climbs by hairpin bends through the forest till it flattens out giving a fine panoramic view of the lake below. A warning notice that this road is 'unsuitable for coaches' confronts the driver. This is a gross understatment as the road is narrow and twisty, and, after the top of the pass, skirts the edge of a deep gorge with a fearsome drop on the left. One harldy expects the quiet Berwyns to present such a hair-raising passage but careful car drivers need have no fear and the road does carry the charm of excitement. It lands you in Bala.

CHAPTER FOUR

THE RED HAIRED BRIGANDS OF MAWDDWY

High up beneath the crags of Aran Mawddwy, a lonely cwm sends down a stream called the Afon Cowarch to join the infant Dovey and send it on its way to the sea.

This mountain retreat was the hideout of a band of red-haired robbers who, for decades terrorized the countryside around, robbing and murdering those who resisted them. Below their lairs, in the village of Dinas Mawddwy, the people locked and barred their doors at night and placed scythes and sharp implements in their wide chimneys against attack from the roof. This was in the reign of Queen Mary, but even as late as the nineteenth century George Borrow, in his travels, found the village a collection of 'filthy huts with fierce-looking red-haired men staggering about, looking like descendants of the robbers of two centuries before'. (Dinas Mawddwy to day is a law-abiding village catering for tourists).

The boldness of these brigands grew with impunity. The officers of the law feared them. Others they bribed. They would drive bunches of stolen cattle across the boundary into the next county where the laws of their own county did not operate and sell them openly in the market. Travellers to West Wales avoid Dinas Mawddwy for fear of attack. 'A place of blue earth and savage men,' they called it. Farmers marked their sheep with the blue earth and the 'savage men' were lead miners.

In desperation, the law-abiding element of the population appealed to the Government and Queen Mary commissioned Lewis Owen, the baron who ruled the region, to raise a force of armed men to make an end of the outlawry.

On a Christmas Eve, the baron and his men surrounded the lairs of the brigands, captured 80 of them and hauled them off for trial. Many were condemned to be hanged and, among these were two youths whose mother pleaded for the life of the younger. The baron refused her plea. He could not make exceptions. On hearing this, the mother screamed her vengeance. 'These yellow breasts', she shouted, 'have given suck to those who will wash their hands in your blood'.

After the trial, the gang plotted their revenge and determined on an ambush. They knew the baron attended the local assizes on a certain day and the route he would take. This led past the present day Brigands Hotel at Mallwyd and followed a deeply-wooded defile where a small stream descended in a deep cwm. This ravine was the place they chose for the ambush, were the road forded the stream; a place where, in any case, the baron's coach would have to slow down. To carry out their plans, the coach would have to stop so they felled trees and blocked the road with them.

Having laid their ambush they hid behind rocks and boulders waiting for the baron's coach and cavalcade. As the baron's men reached the obstruction, they dismounted and went forward to clear it. This was the cue for the brigands to attack. They rose from their hiding places and let loose a shower of arrows into the baron's escort. One of these struck the baron in the face but he drew it out and prepared to defend himself. His son in law drew his sword and stood by him but his escort turned and fled. The robbers now discarded their bows, took up their bills and daggers, dragged the baron from the coach and his son in law from his horse and fell upon them with their weapons. The baron died, pierced by thirty stab wounds and his son in law was overpowered. The old mother's threat had been fulfilled.

The outrage was followed by stern measures. The whole district was combed for the murderers who were either caught and hanged or fled the country.

The site of the ambush is plain today. The road bends sharply as it enters the deep cwm, a bridge spans the stream and the road continues along the steep side of the gorge beyond. Even today the whole place has an air of menace, perhaps haunted by the spirit of the baron. The only indication we have today of the tragic spot are road signs on both sides of the sharp bend.

To remind travellers of the outrage, the Brigands Inn at Mallwyd displays a whole armoury of ancient weapons. And the trade mark of the Woollen Mill at Dinas Mawddwy is a brigand bending a bow.

CHAPTER FIVE

WELSHPOOL

In the days when roads were muddy tracks impassable in Winter and railways had not been dreamed of, it was the rivers that our forefathers looked to for transport. High-masted trows sailed up the Severn bringing trade goods from Gloucester and returning with the produce of the countryside. The limit of navigation on the Severn in those far-off times was Welshpool with its quay at Pool. From here the Welsh flannel went by water to the warehouses of Shrewsbury to be exchanged for the hardware of Coalbrookdale and the coal of Coalport. With the Industrial Revolution, canals proved more reliable than the river and Welshpool and Newtown were linked with industrial England by water till the railways came.

As a Border town Welshpool's history was a history of Border warfare with Gwenwynnyn prince of Powys as custodian of Welsh independence. It was this prince who gave Welshpool its first trading charter in 1263 together with its Monday market. This market persisted all down the centuries to this day.

POWIS CASTLE

There had to be a castle at Welshpool in the ding dong warfare of the Middle Ages. The first castle was erected by Owain ap Gruffydd to hold back the encroaching Border Barons who coveted the fertile lands of the Severn valley. Afterwards, when the place was firmly in the hands of the English it was used to watch out for the raiding Welshmen who came to carry off the fat cattle of England. Many were the forays back and forth of the raiding Welsh and the avenging reprisals of the English. The latter eventually built the great Powys castle to overawe the Welsh. This blocked the way to England along the Severn valley but another, even easier route lay wide open. This was round the back of the Long Mountain and it headed direct to Shrewsbury the ultimate strongpoint of English domination. For hundreds of years the battle front swung back and fore as first the English and then the Welsh were temporary victors. Many an uneasy peace was agreed upon the banks of the Severn at the ford of Rhydwiman, the invasion route of the Welsh raiders. This was where the envoys of the opposing armies met to patch up an agreement with the waters of the river between them to discourage treachery.

But, beyond the river, the English had a long-stop in the strong castle of Montgomery held by that redoubtable Roger Montgomery, the Norman Swordsman and baron.

The great castle of Powis stands today in the rugged strength of its

Red Sandst one towers, whereas the castle of Montgomery, in spite of its inaccessible crag went down in surrender to the troops of Sir Thomas Myddleton in the Civil War.

Powis castle survived the Civil War because it was spared by Cromwell who probably had his reasons for doing so. It could be offered to Sir Thomas Myddleton for his loyalty to Parliament. With the Restoration of Charles II, its future was assured and ever since his day it has been a stately home with its gardens laid out by Capability Brown, its State Rooms open to the public and the tallest tree in Britain, (a Douglas Fir) standing 160 feet in height in its grounds.

Welshpool breathes the air of the sixteenth century and turns its back on Wales, building its houses with English brick instead of Welsh slate and depending, in Georgian times on the weaving of wool for its livelihood. Today, with the Welsh woollen industry dead, it is famous for its market where the farmers roll in from all over Mid-Wales with lorries and trailers full of Welsh cattle and sheep for English buyers.

The Severn hurries by, before becoming a deep lowland river at Pool but Welshpool keeps the river at arms length and is out of reach of its floods. The canal, once a busy waterway, now slumbers weedily on its way to Newtown. Vandalistic moderns have threatened its quiet existence time and again and in places have even filled it in to make a motorway, but there are still long stretches where the fishermen sit on warm summer evenings pulling out a roach here and an eel there. May the conservationists keep the canal.

The bustle of Newtowns is absent from Welshpool which has a historic tradition to maintain and a dignity to preserve. A factory is an anachronism in Welshpool that delights in half-timbered houses and old churches. Royalist traditions reside in the house of 1661 date that still displays the imprecation 'God damn old Oliver'.

I dont want to give the impression that Welshpool is a sleepy town with narrow mediaeval streets. It is not: it is just unhurried and a little Victorian except for the horrible main road traffic that roars through the very middle of it.

THE LITTLE RAILWAY

Take your hats off to the Llanfair Light railway. Except for a modestly salaried manager it is run entirely on voluntary labour.

As a viable undertaking it ran entirely 'under its own steam' until 1956, taking goods and passengers between Welshpool and Llanfair Caereinion. Then the road lorry and the motor bus beat it and it closed. It died but it refused to lie down. Enthusiastic steam railway fans took it over and brought it to life again. When funds were running low and a second closure was impending, the gallant little railway struck a windfall:

it was able to buy cheaply an entire train. As part of German Reparations after the war. A fine new engine built by the French under German occupation and some brand new coaches came into the possession of the railway. The outfit exactly fitted the tracks of the old railway and brought it to vigorous life again. The engine was renamed The Countess but the coaches still bore the livery of the Austrian Alpine railway in which they had served. Some few years ago I was fortunate enough to see this little train leave its terminus for Llanfair Caereinion, served by its enthusiastic volunteers and carrying a crowd of happy children who had come for the trip. It was a heart-warming sight.

Back at Llanfair Caereinion station the restoration of the line was obviously complete with booking office remodelled, a new refreshment cabin and old coaches re-designed as sleeping accommodation for the volunteer helpers.

This 'Great little train of Wales' was in business again.

ROUND ABOUT DOLGELLAU

Thackeray in his travels through Wales once looked for a meal in a certain hotel in Dolgellau. They kept him waiting; so, to pass the time he wrote in the visitors' book:

> If ever you come to Dolgelly,
> Dont stay at the - - hotel.
> There's nothing to put in your belly,
> And no one to answer the bell.

But Thackeray was impatient; he may have spent all day climbing Cadair Idris and was hungry. William Condry, writing about Cadair, says: to make sure of seeing Ireland from the summit, choose a very cold day in midwinter when the air is clear. Personally I prefer a hot day in August when the summit, and the Foxes Path leading to it, is clear of snow, and perhaps, clear of mist as well. The best approach to my thinking is to climb up from the Tal-y-llyn lake via Llyn Cau and descend to Dolgellau for tea down the Foxes Path. The views from the summit, if the weather is clear, are marvellous: Snowdon and all the Welsh peaks; the Wicklow Hills in Ireland and the Clees of Worcestershire if you're lucky. Majestic Cadair, (if not cloud-capped), is grand from the Corris side but even grander from the North in its sheer scarp.

Dolgellau has as long a history as any town in Wales. Its founder, Hywel ap Gruffydd was grandson of that famous Welsh prince Owain Gwynedd, but it was Owain Glyndwr, a few hundred years later who put it on the map. An ironmonger's store called Parliament House today was his headquarters, although Machynlleth boasts the capital from which he proclaimed himself King of Wales.

History resides in the narrow streets and alleys of Dolgellau but, except for layout, little remains of its mediaeval aspect. Its buildings of sombre local slate do not add to its attractive appearance although its Georgian Shire Hall has dignity. Its parish church has the effigy of a fourteenth-century knight although the church dates only from the eighteenth century. (The original 13th century church had to be knocked down to build it). One of the finest historic features of the town is the grand old bridge across the Wnion river. Built in 1638, its narrow 'horse and cart' width was for long a hazard to pedestrians but now at last, it has a footbridge alongside. Built for horses and carts and the squire's four-in-hand, it stands up nobly today under the pounding of thirty-ton lorries.

The Middle Ages speak from Cymmer Abbey, two miles down river. Founded by Owain Gwynedd about the same time as Dolgellau itself, its ruins are unspectacular, judging by what Henry VIII's vandals left at the Dissolution. Whatever the quality of its architecture, its silver Communion Plate was very beautiful. When Thomas Cromwell's wreckers at the Dissolution were sighted, the monks buried it in the ground for safety. Many hundreds of years later, miners digging for gold found it and sold it for fifty shillings. It changed hands several times and was eventually sold for £3,000 and was donated to the National Museum of Wales. A picture showing both chalice and paten is on the wall of Llanelltyd church nearby, which vies in history with the abbey itself: its grand old fifteenth century beams, its ancient stone with the imprint of a pilgrim's foot and its round churchyard outside which Welsh gold miners had bare-fisted bouts with the Cornish miners in the last century.

The old gentry of the district were the Vaughan family of Nannau and Hengwrt. Their fame as collectors of ancient Welsh manuscripts has gone down in history. These manuscripts were finally donated to the National Library of Wales and their literary value is fabulous.

The fame of Dolgellau resides, not in its historical associations but in the rugged beauty of its setting. The glorious Mawddach velley alone would establish its fame but when you add the Precipice Walk, the Torrent Walk and the beautiful Wnion valley you have a portfolio of loveliness that no town in Wales can better.

Since the days when they built sailing ships at Llanelltyd and the tide came up to the town bridge, the old industries of the town have declined. Women and girls no longer spin the wool from local sheep or weave the cloth in their homes, but farmers come from the ends of Wales to buy the Welsh Black cattle sold in Dolgellau market.

In the last century there was a minor Gold Rush that filled the hotels with prospectors and the countryside with hopeful gold diggers. Mines such as the Clogau employed 500 men and tiaras and wedding rings for royalty were made from local gold. But the boom did not last and today the mine workings are derelict and the tunnels flooded. At one time, the great Rio Tinto mining corporation were proposing to dredge the sands of the Mawddach for gold but their plans did not get off the ground.

Opposition from local conservationists was too strong. Would the estuary remain as beautiful if torn up by the iron teeth of excavators? Far better for Dolgellau to retain its natural beauty and be a holiday town for tourists, mountain climbers and fisherman.

DOLGELLAU OF THE GEORGIANS AND THE VICTORIANS

I conclude this description of Dolgellau with snippets from a **Country Quest** article by Brian Slyfield.

A traveller in 1775, Sir Thomas Gery Cullum, calling the place, 'no despicable little town for these parts', bemoans the lack of literary converse in the gentry but adds that at least they are not 'starved with hunger and cold'. He then goes on to say that, in one respect, the inhabitants are more civilized than the English as the gallows on the hill above the town had not been used for 33 years.

Joseph Cradock, writing in 1777, calls Dolgellau, 'This miserable place! there is no street in it; you pass from dungeon to dungeon through a multiplicity of hog yards'.

In 1797, the Rev. Richard Warner of Bath, after footslogging it from Machynlleth, spent the night at the Golden Lion. The next day he wrote, 'We rose earlier than usual after a most comfortless night, during which we had been tormented by fleas and nearly suffocated by the closeness of the room, nine feet by five, into which were crammed two beds, a table and a chair'.

The Rev. William Bingley, visiting Dolgellau in 1801, talks of its' maze of twisting back lanes and alleyways' and of his experiences at the Blue Lion. His bill was 5/-:

Two dinners, (N.B. Bread and butter)	Is.6d
Tea supper and breakfast	Is.0d
Ale	2s.6d

He goes on to describe his host the landlord. Besides being an innkeeper, he was a schoolmaster, a cutter of gravestones and a guide, 'with a considerable taste for ale'.

He speaks of the enormous population of jackdaws among the rooftops that kept him awake in the early mornings. 'Two distinct breeds' he called them: 'Churchmen and Dissenters who never agree except in making a prodigious row'.

CHAPTER 6

ROUND ABOUT MACHYNLLETH

Machynlleth has its own particular charms but none spectacular. It sits in the valley of the turbulent Dovey but its founders placed it sufficiently far from that glorious stream to be out of reach of its angry floods.

Its wide main street bears the imprint of Roman town planners in its spaciousness for it was the high road to their seaport at Pennal, two miles downstream. They probably shipped lead from there back to Rome as the Georgians did in later centuries from Derwenlas on the opposite bank.

In the last century, slate came hurtling down from the quarries of Corris, first for shipment at Derwenlas and later to be loaded on railway trucks at Machynlleth station. The track of the little railway that brought it down across the Dovey can still be seen. In the old days, besides carrying slate, it took Summer tourists to Corris and, from there, horse-drawn wagonettes took them on to the Tal y llyn lake and the foot of Cader Idris. (Perhaps, one day the track will have rails once more, and little steam engines).

The Dovey is famous for its salmon. I once talked to a roadman, leaning on his shovel beside the Severn at Llanidloes. (Roadmen love to talk). I asked him what the Severn salmon were like. 'Poor specimens', he replied. 'Now, your Dovey salmon is a different fish lusty, fat and fighting fit, straight up from the Irish Sea.'

Poachers know the Dovey salmon besides the legitimate fishermen, and the river men know the poachers. At Corris I learned about a local policeman who tried to catch a Dovey poacher at the Dovey bridge. The poacher had a concealed shotgun and when the policeman challenged him he fired and made a horrible mess of the policeman's face.

Machynlleth seems to have a greater claim to the honour of being Owain Glyndwr's capital than Dolgellau. His Parliament House still stands in Maengwyn Street and his tradition has named the Glyndwr Hotel. English domination became intolerable to the Welsh in 1402, and, under Glyndwr, Welshmen rose in revolt. In a cul de sac ravine, not far from Machynlleth, the English force, sent to capture Glyndwr were trapped and slaughtered. The Welshmen swept down from the Hyddgen Crags with flashing swords and fiendish yells while the English were strung out along the narrow gorge. It was a victory of strategy, like his victory at Pilleth. But after six years of glory Wales knew him no more. He established a tradition of Welsh valour on the field of battle but his vision of a united Wales remained a myth. Building on Owain's foundations, Machynlleth became a trading town two hundred years later.

Wealthy merchants like Owen Pugh got rich on the export of wool, hides and skins and built themselves fine houses like the 17th century house in Maengwyn Street. The Welsh gentry are proud of their pedigrees and Owen Pugh was no exception. His house carries the date 1628 and he shows pride in his ancestry by a tree worked in plaster over the chimney breast in the principal room. (Permission to view may be given.)

This, however, is less historic than Owain Glyndwr's Parliament house before mentioned which contains the original building preserved for posterity. Of later date, (17th century), is Plas Machynlleth now housing the Town's Antiquities, the gift to the town of the Londonderry family through the late Marquess of Londonderry. No blood was shed when this family acquired the estate: it came to them by a convenient marriage. In honour of the family the imposing clock tower at the junction of Maengwyn Street was built. Cynics are inclined to indulge their cynicism about its architecture but if you consider it rather noble you probably have Victorian tastes. To me, it extols the Victorian virtue of industry as opposed to pleasure and reminds me of an inscription on the face of a church clock I once saw in Hertfordshire: 'Time flies. Mind your business.'

If the Romans planned the broad Maengwyn Street it was probably in Tudor times that the townspeople took advantage of its spaciousness to hold a street market. At certain recognized times, open-air stalls line both sides of this wide thoroughfare. Many sell their goods on the system known as Dutch Auction others, like the average shopkeeper, but all pay rent to the Town Council for their sites except the gipsies who evade the charge by a mobile stall that they move a foot from time to time. No doubt protests are heard from the regular shopkeepers about evasion of rates but the custom has long been an insitution.

George Borrow, that inveterate foot slogger of the last century stayed the night at the Wynnstay Arms at Machynlleth on his long walk through Wales. He was joined at dinner by a lawyer who had been engaged to defend a poacher accused of spearing salmon in the Dovey. Borrow was interested enough to stay and hear the case when it came before the magistrate. Despite the specious arguments of the lawyer and the innuendos derived from the statements of the keepers who had apprehended the accused poacher, 'that for their evil lifes, they had been driven from Machynlleth to London,' the case went against the lawyer's client and the poacher was fined £4. A certain Lord V. was in the chair and he probably had in mind his own salmon.

Borrow also speaks of the legend of David Gam, sworn enemy of Owain Glyndwr. This individual with a grudge had come to Machynlleth with the threat of stabbing Glyndwr but the latter heard of

18

the threat and clapped Gam into prison.

This version of the Gam affair differs from the version placed near Dolgellau. In this, with false friendship, Glwyndwr and Gam went hunting together and Gam tried to emulate Sir Walter Tyrrell who shot the Red King in the New Forest. He turned his bow on Glyndwr but Glyndwr avoided the arrow and slew Gam with his sword. He then hid the body in a hollow oak.

You can take your choice of these two versions.

Today, the fate of the railway that once carried the Corris slate to England is itself in the balance. The English now roof their houses with tiles, as slate is too dear and British Rail have declared the Machynlleth railway to be uneconomic. The motor car has supplanted the train.

Machynlleth may not look as Mediaeval as Dolgellau but we must not run away with the idea that it dates only from Glyndwr's time. It was sufficiently important in Norman times for it to be given a trading charter and the right to hold a weekly market. So when you see all those stalls on both sides of Maengwyn Street, think of Edward I and his attempts to pacify the Welsh after defeating them. Like Dolgellau, it has no Norman castle so it was probably a law-abiding town even in those exciting times. Today it is a holiday town offering fishing, golf and rambles in glorious scenery. The seaside at Aberdovey is less than ten miles distant and the Tal y llyn steam railway only a little further, all good holiday fare.

CHAPTER SEVEN

MINES OF LEAD AND GOLD

The lead mines of Cardiganshire have been famous for centuries. The Romans who went to Cornwall for tin probably sailed their galleys up the Dovey to Pennal for lead, but it was the invention of gunpowder that started the demand for lead. Lead shot would carry further. Sir Hugh Myddleton, in the 1600's made a great fortune from his Cardiganshire lead mines and spent it all on bringing the New River to London. Thomas Bushell was a great Royalist in the Civil War and from his mining activities he equipped a whole army for Charles I with lead shot smelted at Aberystwyth and money minted there. Horses and carts carried the lead ore to Aberystwyth for 10s. a load until Foden steam waggons took over the job in the late 19th century. Lewis Morris was commissioned by Queen Elizabeth I to manage the lead mines at Esgair Mwn near Ffair Rhos and was getting on well till the local landlords interferred. Viscount Lisburne of Trawscoed and Powell of Nanteos claimed that he was mining on their land, but as the former held an office under the Crown he could not go against Queen Elizabeth's ordinance openly. The pair of them therefore got an unprincipled monster named Herbert Lloyd of Peterwell to do the dirty work of ousting the Queen's man. Getting together a gang of toughs, he attacked the miners, holding a pistol at the head of poor Morris and driving the miners out. The landlords of the 18th century were a law unto themselves. Look at this Herbert Lloyd man. He wanted a field belonging to an old tenant who refused to sell. So Lloyd got his men to let a ram down the old man's chimney in the night. The next day, the ram was found on Shon Philips premises and he was hauled before the court, accused of stealing it. Lloyd was a magistrate and Shon Philip was hanged for theft.

Those were the early days of lead mining when the veins of lead ore were near the surface and easily got. A shepherd would kick a turf and expose the gleam of galena, showing a lode of lead just waiting to be mined. Later on they had to mine deep to get the lead.

There were hundreds of mines all over Cardiganshire, some rich, like the Van mine near Llandiloes, others producing silver as well as lead like the Esgair Hir mine that George Borrow stumbled upon in his walk through Wales.

One of the most productive was the Cwm Ystwyth mine where shafts were not necessary; all the miners had to do was to drive 'levels', (Horizontal tunnels), into the mountain side to strike the lodes.

At this mine the ore-crushing and refining plant is still to be seen as the mine did not close till the early part of the present century.

The great Dylife mine, just over the county border is a good example of the primitive conditions in which the miners worked with hammer and pick. This mine employed 500 men who lived in barracks from Monday till Friday, sleeping in the beds vacated by the shift off duty: beds that were infested with lice. The beds were never cold. And this in spite of John Bright and Cobden, the social reformers being part owners of the mine.

This mine was the scene of a foul murder. The mine blacksmith began to fail to come home at week-ends and stories reached his wife that he was having an affair with a woman at the mine. One week-end, she took her young daughter and visited the mine to find out. The man admitted his guilt but promised to reform and come home with her. On the way, he murdered her and the child and threw their bodies down a mine shaft.

They were found by a miner who spread the information around. The blacksmith was summoned to an improvised court of his mates and condemned to be hanged in chains. They made him forge his own headpiece and erected a gallows tree, where he was duly hanged. Mr. Will Richards, an old lead miner of Aberhosan told me the story of how he dug beneath where the gallows had stood and found the headpiece that had been buried there. It is now in St. Fagans museum, a token of the rough justice of the 18th century.

The ruins of the miners' church are still to be seen at Dylife but the three chapels and the school have been raised to the ground with the barracks and everything except the pub. This still functions and, according to a story I heard, is well patronized by steady drinkers from local towns.

All the old Cardiganshire mine buildings are now in ruins but one. This is the Llywernog mine near Ponterwyd which has been restored by Peter Harvey, an enterprising man from Aberaeron who has opened it as a tourist attraction with miners' equipment and reconstructed buildings showing how the lead was won.

Old William Edwards of Cruglas and Mr. Caradoc Edwards of Strata Florida both told me about the old mines round Ffair Rhos and Pontrhydygroes. The former was 72 when I spoke to him; (May he still be alive). He had worked in the Esgair Mwyn mine; ninepence a day as a boy and eight and twopence a day as a skilled miner. 'There's plenty of lead left in that mine', He said, 'only waiting for modern equipment'.

The Romans mined for gold at Pumsaint and sent home to their wives and sweethearts gold bangles and bracelets. The workings have been busy all down the ages since. I once employed a mason who had worked there.

21

The great Welsh Gold Rush, however, was in Meirionethshire near Dolgellau. There were two big mines, each employing about 500 men and royal wedding rings and coronets were made from the gold they produced. One of these mines was near Bont Ddu between Dolgellau and Barmouth and the other in the forest of Coed y Brenin in the romantic valley of the Mawddach. (The glorious waterfalls of Pistyll Gain and Mawddach are on the way there). The gold Rush, however, did not last. Both mines are now derelict.

Like gold, lead mining often brought out the worst in men. In the 1700's a man named John Ball arrived at Aberystwyth penniless but he knew his way about. By dint of toadying to the gentry, cheating the miners and blackmailing the shipowners, he became himself a shipowner and owner of much property in the town. He died a wealthy man. Others like Thomas Bonsall used their lead revenues to bring benefits to Aberystwyth. He promoted building, took part in the government of the town and was an active justice of the peace.

CHAPTER EIGHT

THE WOOLLEN INDUSTRY OF WALES

The manufacture of wool is traditional in Wales. Sheep have grazed on the rough pastures of Welsh moorlands from earliest recorded times and peasant women have spun their wool in their homes from the days of the native princes. The monks of Strata Florida abbey kept thousands of sheep on the lands granted them by the princes of their day and by judicious breeding improved the quality of the wool. From earliest times, the women of Dolgellau knitted 'webs' from their local wool and traded them down the Mawddach and the women of Bala sat by the hour on the sunny slopes of their mediaeval 'tomen' gossiping and knitting as they talked. English traders took away the stockings and socks they produced by pack donkeys to sell in the Border counties where the warmth and wearing qualities of Welsh wool had a long reputation.

As time went on, machinery replaced the spinning wheel and the hand loom, and little valley industries sprang up wherever a mountain stream could supply the power to drive the water wheel. These water-powered factories kept going until Hargreaves, Arkwright and Compton invented the power spinning jenny and the power loom that could spin many threads at once and weave larger cloths. For many years the steam-driven mills of Yorkshire failed to displace the Welsh water-driven factories and, as late as the 1920's and the latter part of the nineteenth century the water mills held their own. At the turn of the century there were 23 water-driven mills in the Velindre-Drefach valley of Carmarthenshire all busy and the operatives even going 'on strike' for more wages on one occasion. All except two have since closed down and even these have been obliged to use more modern machinery and produce modern cloth and tapestries. The days when miners and farm workers wore grey flannel shirts and their women red flannel petticoats are long past. Here and there, however, one of these old water mills survives. There is one still busy, driven by the Clattwr at Capel Dewi still knitting socks, (of which I have a pair), but also obliged to adapt its machinery to modern fabrics. Otherwise, the 'felins' and 'pandys' of yesteryear are today mere names. Ancient mills that once employed hundreds of hands stand stark and silent in scores of Welsh valleys or have been taken over as furniture warehouses or confectionery stores. Along with the stone-ground flour mills they are sadly relics of the past. Except when reconditioned to meet a modern demand for wholemeal flour as at Cwm Cou near Newcastle Emlyn. Where adapted to produce modern fabrics, these old woollen mills still thrive, especially when their products are supplemented with those of old Welsh Crafts.

23

The Derw mill of Pentrecourt Wandysul started as a water mill, then it was driven by a Blackstone oil engine and now by electricity. It still does a thriving trade in modern fabrics. The Meirion mills of Dinas Mawddwy was probably working when the Brigands of Mallwyd terrorized the countryside. Today its products are sold nationwide. Its emblem is the drawn bow of the brigands. The old water-wheel now stands idle beside the mill at Cwm Duad but the mill still functions as a Craft Shop.

World War I and Hilter's War gave a much needed fillip to the stagnating woollen mills of Wales. The mill at Newcastle Emlyn, for instance, produced thousands of yards of khaki cloth for the uniforms of the British army and the mills of Drefach Velindre were equally busy.

A sad memory attaches to an old mill at Drefach. It was bought with all its old machinery but sound buildings by a Pole named Bridlik. He was old when he came to Wales but he brought with him great expertise in the dyeing of fabrics.

The poor old chap had given up the weaving by the time I knew him and, without a wife to look after him, was 'pigging it' in an old shed surrounded by rolls of unsaleable cloth. He cooked his meals on an old oil stove and this was his ending. While he was sleeping in bed, the stove went on fire and he was burned to death. A tragic ending for a man of talent in the manufacture of woollens.

Much larger centres of the woollen industry in Mid-Wales were found in Llanidloes and Newtown. In the last century, big factories arose in both these towns producing woollen cloth for export to England The trade from Newtown was so considerable that a canal was made to that town from Oswestry to bring coal to the factories and take the cloth to Shrewsbury. Here, at Newtown was born that great industrial philanthropist, Robert Owen, who became the father of the cooperative movement of that day. He is honoured by a statue in the town and by a museum displaying all the facets of the now decayed woollen industry. The big factories that once turned out the woollens and flannels in both towns are now silent or turned over to modern industries and the canal is now choked with water weeds. Llanidloes was, in 1839, the centre of the Chartist movement demanding industrial reforms and economic justice for the factory worker. There were street marches and riots and, as the police were powerless to restore order the local militia were brought in. Even the London police had to be brought in to disperse the crowds.

The mayor of the town gave up and was found hiding under the bed. The revolt was exacerbated by the calling in of the London police but finally it subsided with the ringleaders being transported to Australia. The peaceful little town of Llanidloes bears no marks of mob violence today and its mills are silent. Newtown, with many new industries has enough to do to mind its own business. But it hasn't forgotten Robert Owen.

In the early 1900's Welsh flannel commanded a sale in Mediterranean countries and, as far afield as Argentina. Paternalistic slave owners of Georgia and Texas bought Welsh flannel for their cotton-field slaves. In Britian, the Duke of Wellington's army was clothed in Welsh woollens. Newtown, in those times had 35 Spinning Mills and 82 weaving factories. The workers were paid eleven shillings a week but from this payment was deducted the wholesale cost of clothing their families.

The distinctive product of Welsh mills today is double woven tapestry. It is characteristic of Wales, especially in woven bed-covers and is especially attractive as it lends itself to intricate designs in beautiful colours.

CHAPTER NINE

LLANGURIG

IN THE Dark Ages there was a saint called Curig. Since his youth he had been a warrior at the court of his prince and famed for his expertise with the sword and the mace. In his day Christianity was struggling to make headway against paganism and St. David's missionaries converted him to the new religion. He was loth, however, to abandon his fame on the field of battle and he wandered to his Eisteddfa, (seat), at the top of the pass and sat down to do a big think. After wrestling with his conscience all day he was won over to Christ so he laid aside his weapons and joined the army of the Lord. Filled with his new enthusiasm, he went down the valley and founded a Christian church at Llangurig. The church carries his name today.

Centuries later, the monks of Strata Florida used the road through Llangurig to reach their sheep grazings in the Ystwyth valley and centuries after that, this old road was used to reach the lead mines of Cardiganshire. A mining engineer named Francis Thompson travelled that way from Derbyshire to carry out repairs at a mine called Esgair Mwn. He was unsure of the way so the landlord of the pub at Llandiloes where he stayed, provided him with a guide who carried a stout staff to deal with footpads along the road. Thompson rode his mare and the guide trotted along beside him. When they reached Llangurig, they took the mountain road to the Ystwyth valley. (The road over the Plinlimon Pass had not been made at that time). Descending to the gorge of a strong tributary of the Ystwyth, where a ford led across the boulder-strewn bed of the river, the guide leaped up behind the engineer and rode across on the horses's back. Today, the rough track across the mountains is tarmacked as far as the ford and I was told that Montgomeryshire were prepared to bridge the ford if Cardiganshire on the other side would continue the tarmac to the Ystwyth. The Cardis were not prepared and the ford is unbridged today.

Leaving Francis Thompson to complete his journey to the lead mines, we return to Llangurig and take the main road to where the Wye breaks out of its mountain fastnesses at Pont Rhydgaled. Here lived Captain Bennett Evans whose family were patrons of St. Gurig's church at Llangurig and have inscribed plaques on its walls. The Captain was a great sheep man and a pioneer in grazing Welsh Black cattle on his mountain pastures which he improved by spreading fertilizers from aeroplanes. Today his son carries on the tradition selling thousands of sheep every Autumn from his mountain grazings.

When the lead mine fever was at its height and the great Van mine near Llanidloes was producing abundantly, they built a railway from Llandiloes to Llangurig, presumably with the idea of extending it to Cwmystwyth to export the lead from that flourishing mine. Only the track remains today, but the ancient church remains with the tradition of St. Curig who founded it. The bards of old styled him Curig Farchog, (the knight), and after his conversion, Curig Lwyd, (the blessed). It seems he came from Brittany where they called him Kirik and the day of his death, (A.D. 547), is still celebrated there. The Welsh Prince of that time Maelgwyn Gwynedd, gave him the land on which to build his church, and, for his piety, the monks canonized him and made him a bishop.

His cell, (church), became a 'Clas' and the lords of Arwystli became his patrons. Centuries later, in 1164, the abbey of Cistercian monks at Strata Florida was founded and the church and lands of St. Curig were added to the possessions of the new abbey. For 350 years, the monks of Strata Florida enjoyed the sheep grazings round Llangurig and travelled back and forth caring for their sheep and enjoying the revenues of the wool clip. Even the notorious King John remitted the duty on the wool they produced, probably to atone for his own dissolute life.

At the Dissolution came the blow. The abbey at Strata Florida was dissolved, its lands sold to the highest bidder and its fine buildings razed to the ground. This vandalism was accompanied by senseless destruction. The gold-adorned crozier of the saintly bishop was burned, the font slung out to be used as a pig trough and everything of beauty destroyed.

With the Restoration a new era began. The holy vessels were restored, the now damaged font was replaced, new bells were hung in 1700 and in 1740 the lych gate was built. Even so, a distinguished visitor to the church in 1828 described it as 'rude and plain within and without'. By that time, it had a beautiful rood screen and another visitor spoke of this as 'elegantly designed'.

Sadly, the church was to undergo a further vandalism at the hands of Victorian 'restorers'. The rood screen and loft were taken way and the woodwork given away.

But, even today, the beauty of the church remains in the lovely stained glass windows and its antiquity in the fourteenth-century tower.

It is not possible in this short description to convey the present day loveliness of this historic church but a very full description is to be found in the leaflet that may still be available in the church.

CLOCHFAEN

'Gay, trim and pleasant to frequent,
Is Clochfaen Court on the winding Wye'
So wrote Huw Arwystli in 1500

I bring in Clochfaen because the Lords of Clochfaen have been patrons of Llangurig church all down the centuries. In 1171, King Henry II granted to Prince Rhys the Lordship of Llangurig and through Rhy's descendants the Clochfaen estate came into the possession of the Lloyd family. From that time, they remained in possession till 1927 when it was inherited by a gentleman named Hinde, who promptly changed his name to Lloyd of Clochfaen. It was this gentleman who restored Llangurig church in 1875 at the cost of £11,000.

From an article in Country Quest by Audrey c. Stirk, (which I quote), it appears that the Lloyd family were a line of warriors all down the ages, fighting, strangely enough, on Cromwell's side in the Civil War. With Cromwell victorious and his commissioners assessing fines on Royalists, it would seem that Lloyd linked by marriage with the Fowlers of Abber cwm hir might have been responsible for these lines:
Radnorsheer, poor Radnorsheer,
Never a park and never a deer, Never a squire worth five hundred a year,
But Richard Fowler of Abbey cwm hir.

Clochfaen today is still a gentleman's residence but the ancient mansion was burned down in 1760.

CHAPTER TEN

PARSONS BRIDGE

Sitting beside the main road from the famous Devils Bridge to Ponterwyd is an ancient church. It doesn't look so ancient because its marks of antiquity were lost in a restoration in the last century. It dates, however, from the days of pagan worship when Druidism was the religion in Wales. The Druids surrounded their places of worship with a ring of huge boulders, set up on end. Of these, only four remain here today. When Christianity came to Wales the priests grafted the new religion on to the old and to ease the change retained the ancient stones of the Druids.

When Christianity had taken root and the monastery of Strata Florida became a place of pilgrimage, the church happened to be on the pilgrim route to the abbey. Pilgrims brought offerings to the sacred abbey. In return the monks established here a rest-house or hospice for the comfort and convenience of the pilgrims and called the place Ysbyty Cynfyn, (the hospice of Cynfyn, a local patron of the abbey).

At that time, the abbey owned vast sheep grazings in the country around and the monks themselves used the hospice when on their journeys visiting their sheep farms. Then came the Normans bringing the Roman Catholic religion and their Knights Templars took over the running of the hospice.

At the Dissolution of the abbeys, Henry VIII sold the abbey lands to the highest bidder and pocketed the money. But sheep remained the mainstay of the economy although under new owners.

Each of these owners had a distinguishing earmark to identify his sheep but, as the grazings were largely unfenced, one man's sheep often got mixed up with the sheep of another. These were sorted out at shearing time and it was the parson's job to supervise the sorting. He would stand on top of the flat-toppped Druid stone and direct his assistant to return strayed sheep to their proper owners. Using the stone as a pulpit, he would also deliver an appropriate sermon to his flock assembled below, reminding them of the wickedness of stealing another man's sheep.

In those days, the church had no parson; the services were taken by the vicar of Llanbadarn Fawr who came on a pony to do his office. To reach the church, he had to cross the Rheidol river which flows about a quarter of a mile away. In those days, the river was spanned by a couple of rough-hewn planks with a hand-rail. The parson tied up his pony, crossed the bridge, took the service and collected his pony on his return. Thus the bridge took the name: Parson's Bridge.

29

Those were leadmining days. A lead mine stood on the bank of the river near the bridge and the miners crossed the rough bridge on their way to work.

A famous traveller of the last century also crossed the bridge on his Journey through Wales. He was George Borrow and, while his main object was to attend service at the church, he also wanted to see the famous bridge. So he got hold of a Welshman to take him. The final descent to the river is very steep and slippery, so Borrow refused to trust his legs. Casting his dignity aside, he slid down on his bottom. 'You will spoil your trousers, Sir' warned the guide but Borrow liked his own way. At the bottom, the river foamed and surged through a narrow slit in the rocks and it was in fear and trepidation that Borrow followed his guide across the plank bridge. Returning, he was faced with the task of climbing the slope down which he had slid. This, to the amazement of his guide, he did on his hands and knees.

Today an iron footbridge spans the fearsome gorge in place of the plank bridge but the torrent of the river is much diminished. The water now passes through pipes underground to feed the turbines of the hydroelectric station in Cwm Rheidol; only 'compensation water' remains in the Rheidol.

Back at the church we may meet Mr. Alfred Jenkins, self-appointed warden, sexton and groundsman of church, churchyard and indeed of the path that leads to the bridge itself. He keeps the whole place, clean tidy and trimmed up. He took me into the church to show me that many of the old features had been retained at the last restoration in 1836. The old oak beams of the roof were still there along with the wall plaques inscribed with the Creed, the Lord's Prayer and the Ten commandments. 'There used to be a gallery at the West End', said Mr. Jenkins. 'In those days there were large congregations of farmers and lead miners that occupied the body of the church. The gallery held the younger element, some of whom were unruly . They aimed ripe sloes on to the bald pates of the old men below till removed by the sexton.

Meyrick the Historian of 1805 speaks of an octangular font of stone in his time but the font I saw was delightfully carved from wood. According to Mr. Jenkins, it came from East Anglia and had been presented to the church by himself and his brother.

Taking me into the churchyard, he showed me the grave of a family of quads, three girls and a boy born and died in 1856. Their father died of typhus, a common scourge in those days. Another grave occupied the top corner of the churchyard: the grave of a suicide. He left his motorcycle at the top of Plinlimmon Pass and disappeared. In spite of a reward of £5, it was six weeks before he was found on the mountain shot through the head, his body lying in a stream.

Historian Meyrick speaks of old pastimes in which the church was cleared of furniture and used for local wrestling bouts on certain days in the year. Often the competitors stayed all night, watched by old champions to see fair play, along with miners' wives and daughters who cheered on their favourites.

CHAPTER ELEVEN

A GLORIOUS VALLEY. A PATERNALISTIC SQUIRE.

No one could call the Ystwyth an angry river as it ripples peacefully over its stony bed near Trawscoed but see it in Winter when the mountain snows have melted and it surges down its broad valley in a deep yellow flood. In Summer, its gentle stream remains within the bounds of Nature but in Winter it can be a raging torrent bearing on its billowy bosom great tree trunks and the carcases of sheep that have perished in the mountain snows. Its deep valley trenches through the wooded mountains revealing the lodes of lead ore that come to the surface along its valley sides with old mines like Grogwnion still gaping in rocky tunnels where hundreds of men once sweated to extract the ore.

Beyond the broad valley, a vast mass of rock obstructs the river which, in centuries of erosion has cut its way down in a deep narrow gorge. Beyond it we reach Pontrhydygroes a lead miners' village that looks down into the gorge with the old miners' cottages hanging on the slopes. The river is crossed at Pontrhydygroes by a stone bridge that carries the history of the river's tantrums. When it got washed away, they engaged a local builder to rebuild it. He had nearly done so when a teriffic flood came down the river ruining his work. The poor chap had spent all the money he contracted to spend and when he was faced with the necessity of rebuilding the flood damage he was appalled at the prospect. It would ruin him. His council were sympathetic, however, and they gave him a grant to cover his loss. (See 'Hafod Mansion')

DEVILS BRIDGE

Parson's Bridge is a mere prelude to something far more spectacular: Devils Bridge. Here, at the bottom of a deep chasm runs the torrent of the Mynach, (the Monks' river). Legend goes back to the days before the gorge was spanned by any bridge and the custodian of the fearsome rocky slit was the devil. He claimed, as his victim the first to cross the yawning gulf. An old lady had a cow which, by devious paths, had strayed to the far side of the chasm. She feared to cross to get it back, knowing that the devil would seize her as she crossed. So she called her little dog and sent him across to round up the cow. The devil's powers, she knew, could only be used on humans so the dog went across unharmed.

When the monks built their abbey at Strata Florida, they had to cross the gulf to visit their sheep pastures on the other side. For their convenience and safety, the abbot built a bridge over the torrent and called it Pont y gwr drwg (Bridge of the devil). Around Tudor times, this bridge had an evil reputation as the haunt of a gang of robbers who preyed on travellers passing along the old monks' route. The most

notorious of these were called 'The wicked children' or the Plant de Bat: two brothers and a sister: all robbers and murderers. They lived in a cave below the gorge and it was some years before they were smoked out and hanged at Rhayader. To prevent a repetition of this lawlessness and ease the passage of travellers, a second bridge was built above the monks' bridge in the 1700's and this is still to be seen. When wheeled traffic became general, a third bridge was built at the highest level: the iron bridge we cross today. Thus the three bridges carry the history of the gorge from Mediaeval times till today.

George Borrow crossed the bridge, descended into the gorge to see the 'boiling cauldron at the bottom where the waters whirl before escaping through a 'horid slit in the rocks'.

Today you pass through a turnstile and descend to view this wonder of Nature by a rocky Jacobs Ladder with handrails for your safety. You can also descend on the other side of the bridge for a view of the three bridges superimposed and the succession of waterfalls by which the Mynach escapes to join the Rheidol down below.

Devils Bridge today is a honeypot for tourists and visitors. They come in their thousands by car and by the narrow-gauge Devils Bridge railway from Aberystwyth. There is a nice cafe by the bridge with holiday shops and a post office cafe. Tourists are well catered for. Then there is the Hafod Arms Hotel dating from the days of the paternalistic squire Thomas Johnes who built the mansion. When stage coaches brought visitors from England the hotel was an inn where travellers sat round a fire of logs with players on the harp to entertain them. The welcome of the hotel today is as warm as it was in stage coach days but today its hospitality appeals to the more affluent.

CHAPTER TWELVE

HAFOD MANSION AND THE ROBBERS CAVE

To reach the site of the famous Hafod Mansion, it is best to take the Trawscoed road, (B4340), from Aberystwyth and turn L beside the Ystwyth river for Pontrhydygroes after the Trawscoed Mansion. The road along the river is one of charm and loveliness, wooded along one side and open to the wide flood-plain of the Ystwyth on the other. In Summer, the river prattles inoffensively along its stony bed but in winter when the melting snows of the mountains send down their angry floods, it fills the valley with a yellow torrent from bank to bank, carrying tree trunks ripped from their rootholds and the carcases of dead sheep that have perished in the snow. Cart loads of lead ore, destined for the holds of ships in Aberystwyth harbour once went this way from the mines in the valley and of Pontrhydygroes, the mining village we are coming to.

As we approach the village, the valley narrows to a gorge and the river flows in a rocky slit, hidden beneath a canopy of trees.

The village of Pontrhydygroes was a miners' village with its miners' cottages perched on impossible ledges along the steep sides of the valley. At the end of the village is the Miners Arms, now an hotel, but once an inn where the miners once washed the poisonous lead dust from their throats in copious pints of beer. (But the dust stayed in their lungs to kill them at forty). At a bend in the road, steps lead up to the rear of a house that used to be the mine office. Here through a window, now blocked up, Mr. Nantcarrow, the Cornish mine manager, paid the miners their weekly wages.

Passing through the village, (which boasts a public toilet), you reach the bridge over the Ystwyth, and, turning R, the iron gates of the old Hafod mansion are before you. Through the gates, the road is lined with rhododendrons, sign of squirely prestige, and, in half a mile the road forks L to reach the site where the mansion stood. What was left of the mansion after the fire, has been raised to the ground in vandalistic fashion to make a caravan park although a native told me it deserved preservation.

Here, at the beginning of the last century, lived Thomas Johnes, a paternalistic landlord who spent the wealth he inherited from Shropshire ironworks in making a glorious home for his wife and daughter and in improving the lot of his tenants. He spared no expense in building his luxurious mansion in the Gothic style. Meyrick, the historian, who saw it at the turn of the century went into raptures describing it: 'Large and capacious, but light and airy, with a music room, summer and winter dining rooms, a drawing room and a library full of priceless books.

34

Meyrick speaks of a conservatory, one hundred and sixty feet in length, lighted from above and filled with exotic plants and flowers. The library was octagonal in shape, with a dome for lighting. The precious books included old Welsh manuscripts and Froissart's chronicles. The writer, Elizabeth Inglis Jones, has also described the mansion in her book 'Peacocks in Paradise', (Galloways £1), telling also the tragic story of Johnes's beloved daughter Mariamne. Johnes filled his beautiful valley with trees, planting them by the million. Most of them have since been burned to make charcoal for smelting lead but the mantle of the great agriculturalist has been assumed today by the Forestry Commission who have clothed the valley anew with trees.

THE ROBBERS CAVE

Passing below the mansion site, you are in Forestry Commission territory so you must conduct yourselves as you would on the property of a valued friend. Pass through the arch of rock created by Johnes, cross the concrete bridge and look for a wooden hut beside the road. From the hut, walk up the ride between the trees and turn L at the top. (It is best to wear boots or wellingtons here). Follow the path along the edge of a gorge where a stream hurries down to join the Ystwyth. The path is rocky in places but, in ten minutes, it will take you to a semi-circular wall of rock from which the stream comes. Here is the entrance to the 'cave'. This is more of a tunnel through the rock made by the lead miners of old. The tunnel is about twenty yards long and it ends overlooking a chasm into which a waterfall descends down a sheer rock face. Here was the robbers' hideout, when, in Tudor times, they haunted the Ystwyth valley and robbed passing travellers. George Owen talks about them in his book on Pembrokeshire. 'Having squared the Sheriff', he says, 'they would appear openly at fairs and sales with bunches of cattle they had stolen in an adjoining county'.

Having seen the 'cave' and made a mental estimate of the chances of escape for the robbers if cornered there by the law officers, return to the car and drive along to the bridge over the Ystwyth and the dam on the river constructed by Johnes. Then follow the road round an elbow bend to the upper gate to the estate. When back on the tarmac, turn L and visit the church that Johnes built.

It would seem that some evil spirit attended every effort Johnes made to make an earthly paradise out of a Welsh valley for the church also went up in flames and, with it, a monument the sculptor Chantry carved as a memorial to the death of Johnes's much loved daughter. The fire broke the monument in pieces and the fragments are preserved today behind a wire screen.

CHAPTER THIRTEEN

ONLY A POOR TRAMP. A TRAGEDY OF THE MOUNTAINS

Ffair Rhos is a tiny hamlet along the road from Strata Florida to Devils Bridge. It has no importance today except as a centre for Sheep Dog Trials where shepherds compete for the palm of excellance in handling sheep dogs. A century and more ago and cattle were driven from Wales to England 'on the hoof', its importance was known throughout Mid-Wales as the point to which farmers brought their cattle and sheep to be assembled in droves for the long journey across the mountains. There were no tolls to pay on the mountains as there were on the turnpike roads so the mountain route was popular with the drovers. As people gathered in crowds at these annual fairs, the opportunity to sell goods like cloth and fabrics attracted the packmen bringing cottons from Manchester and silks from Macclesfield. They made the journey in the opposite direction with their pack ponies and donkeys and sold their goods in the fair. Thus the route across the mountains which was originally pioneered by the monks of Strata Florida was well known and well used. It headed for Rhayader where the dealers and drovers completed their purchases and made up their droves. The track was rough and bleak, sometimes crossing rocky outcrops sometimes diverging to avoid the morasses of peat hags and always at a high elevation. At intervals, cairns of stones marked the route as guideposts in mist.

Pedlars and travellers to and from the lead mines used the route along with the tramping fraternity, but not in winter when there was risk of snow.

In the winter of 1929, a poor tramp arrived at Ffair Rhos intending to cross the barren wastes to return to England. He called at a cottage in the hamlet asking for food. The lady supplied him, but when he announced his intention to cross the mountains, she pointed to the sky and warned him of the threat of snow. He refused to listen and set off up the mountain track. When he reached the Teifi Pools the blizzard overtook him so he sheltered behind a rock waiting for the storm to pass. Instead of passing, the blizzard increased in fury and the very track by which he had come was blotted out. He drew his old coat about him and waited, half frozen with the cold. As night came on the cold took possession of his whole body, but, strangely, he felt it less and less and grew drowsy. Presently he fell asleep, but it was the sleep of death. He did not wake.

The snow lasted for days but the mountains were covered for weeks and no one knew that the poor tramp was lying in his snowy grave miles from the nearest house.

After a fortnight, the snow cleared sufficiently for the mountain post-man to make his round. He came across the tramp's body lying behind the rock, his face and hands ravaged by crows. Searching his pockets, the postman found the remains of the food he had tried to eat, three copies of Old Moore's Almanack and eightpence halfpenny.

Back at Ffair Rhos, he told his sad story, but no one would undertake to bring the body down for burial or pay the cost of a funeral. Eventually a few kindly farmers put their heads together, took up a horse and gambo and, by night they fetched the body down. In the darkness, they carried it to Strata Florida Abbey, lifted it over the churchyard wall and left it on sacred ground. Gradually the story got around, a rough coffin was made and a slate slab was found that may have been intended for some notable person in the Middle Ages. With money subscribed by charitable persons, the poor tramp was given an honourable burial, and, on the slab, a village artist carved the following epitaph:

UNKNOWN
He died upon the hillside drear,
Alone where snow was deep.
By strangers he was carried here,
Where princes also sleep.

The Teifi Pools today have been deepened to provide a water supply for Cardiganshire but their rugged setting remains. How many of the fishermen who motor up the new tarmac road, know its winter hazards or have heard the story of the poor tramp! His grave can still be seen not far from the wall of the churchyard where they buried him.

CHAPTER FOURTEEN

RHAYADER AND THE ELAN VALLEY

You dont visit Rhayader to 'take the waters' or to visit ancient castles; you call at Rhayader because it is on the way to the Elan Valley. We have spoken elsewhere of the glorious lake, (I refuse to call it a 'reservoir'), of Vyrnwy created in the spacious days of Queen Victoria and now we will talk about the equally beautiful Elan Valley.

As with Liverpool, the great city of Birmingham needed a constant supply of pure water and, like Liverpool, Birmingham went to Wales to find it. They found it in the river Elan, a major tributary of the Wye. This tributary they dammed with three great dams, creating three lovely lakes. Along their shores they planted forests of mountain-loving trees as did Liverpool at Vyrnwy. They copied Liverpool, too, by building a 70-mile pipe-line to carry the water to their city. Again, they copied Liverpool in building their great dams of masonry blasted from the bowels of adjoining mountains; great blocks of stone, each trimmed to shape by the diligent labour of hundreds of skilled masons. The unskilled work was done by crowds of Irishmen brought over from Dublin and housed in barracks. They were a wild lot of men whose greatest fun was poaching salmon in the Wye at Rhayader. My father was schoolmaster at New Radnor and the police sergeant of the village had served his time at Rhayader when these uncontrollable Irishmen were most active. In our schoolhouse kitchen, I would sit open-mouthed as a boy listening to this magnificent sergeant resplendent in his tight-fitting uniform and silver buttons as he related stories of his encounters with the Irish poaching gangs. Stationed in Rhayader, he was called out night after night to do battle with his truncheon against the sticks and cudgels of the wild Irish. The fights were whole-hearted and no quarter given and the victory was not always with the police. A twenty-pound salmon hanging from a policeman's door-knob the next morning was the token of undefeated defiance.

Thus the great dams rose from the rock beds of the gorges and the Welsh water destined for Birmingham crept up the sides of the new reservoirs as architects designed the tasteful castellations of the dam structures. With Victorian love of natural beauty the dams were made to blend with the rugged character of their setting.

In course of time, Birmingham's appetite and need for Welsh water outgrew the capacity of the original reservoirs. The city had to think again. Luckily the answer was already in their hands.

The great tributary, the Claerwen, was not being fully used. It could provide storage capacity that would be equal to the combined capacity of all three original reservoirs. And so, a fourth great dam was built; this time of concrete, not of masonry, as the local stone was unsuitable. It was opened after the second World War by Queen Elizabeth II. And now, even after this great addition to her water supplies, Greater Birmingham is looking to the future. The highest of the three original reservoirs is not being fully exploited; the height of its dam could be doubled and a vast reservoir could be created; a reservoir that would extend to the Ystwyth watershed and even capture some of the Ystwyth water. The scheme is ambitious, but, so far, the project has only been mooted. If it came to fruition, the old coaching road from Rhayader to Aberystwyth would be under the water and would have to be moved higher up the hillside. I have nostalgic recollections of this old stage coach road as I travelled along it with car and trailer in the days when it was innocent of tarmac. The going was just possible but it had been neglected since the toot of the coachman's horn was last heard and the gulleys were rough.

In the days when the Elan Valley reservoirs were constructed, the flooding of valleys and the consequent drowning of mountain farms caused less concern than it does today. Some of the valleys drowned by modern reservoirs have no particular claims to scenic beauty but the Clearwen valley was different: it had the charm of rocks and woodland. Here, in the mansion of Nantgwillt lived the poet Shelley with his ladylove Harriet. When the waters of the Caban coch reservoir are sufficiently low the walls of this old mansion can still be seen.

RHAYADER

Leaving this glorious land of lakes and rocky gorges we follow the Birmingham pipe-line down to Rhayader, the rendezvous of the thousands of tourists who come each summer to see the works of man in the setting of Welsh beauty. (And let it be said that, despite the howls of derision from Conservationists, the beauty of the Elan Valley has been enhanced rather than destroyed by Birmingham's reservoirs).

And so we come to Rhayader beautified by the valley and cataracts of the lovely Wye: Cataracts that gave the town its name. It is a town of hotels, guest houses and craft shops, the modern paraphernalia of tourism.

We need not discount the claims of its handbook on the beauties of its Waun Capel park. (There is amour propre even in tourists brochures); but even a curmudgeon could hardly fail to find natural beauty in Rhayader, especially if he travels up the Wye to its junction with the Marteg or down the Wye gorge past its junction with the Elan.

For the caravan-minded, (and, after all they are a Nature-loving breed), there is a discreetly-hidden caravan park beside the Wye and for equestrian types there is pony-trekking amid grand scenery.

No ancient castle dominates the local scene in Rhayader and even Leland prefers to talk about the scenery of the Teifi Pools, but, in Queen Mary's time the town had magistrates who did their job religiously. They hanged the Plan de Bat, the robbers who terrorized Devils Bridge.

CHAPTER FIFTEEN

HEALING WATERS

Pre-eminent among the 'Wells' towns of Wales is Llandrindod. Even in the days of the Georges when the lumbering stage coach along rutty roads was the only means of public transport, the fashion of Bath filtered through to Wales and sufferers from all sorts of ailments began to flock to Llandrindod to take the waters. In Victorian times the fitful stream of summer visitors, (The roads were too bad in winter), became a flood and the town was bursting its seams with ten times its winter population. Red brick hotels and boarding houses mushroomed overnight and the Pump House was thronged with visitors. Choleric colonels whose blood was over-diluted with whisky sought relief from rheumatic pains and dutifully swilled the obnoxious waters through their systems in the fond hope of a cure. Sufferers from unindentifiable ailments not listed in the medical calendar were advised by their doctor to 'take to the waters'. At Llandrindod the chalybeate waters were not too obnoxious but at Llanwrtyd Wells the waters were impregnated with Sulphuretted Hydrogen and their smell alone was sufficient to deter all but the credulous faithful. And yet I was told that, not only the affluent gentry but the common people came to Llanwrtyd in such vast numbers that they had to sleep ten to a room in the cheaper boarding houses.

Llangammarch Wells had a special attraction for heart sufferers. Its spring was impregnated with Barium Chloride, reputed to be a sovereign remedy for heart disease. Then there was Builth Wells, where, if visitors found the waters distasteful or ineffective, they could at least enjoy the beauties of the lovely Wye.

Of all these 'watering place', Llandrindod was the Queen and when the railway reached the town, its success was assured. It acquired a certain cachet of superiority that appealed to the affluent gentry: it was a resort for the 'best' people with the more aristocratic afflications. Even when I visited the town not many years ago, it was possible to buy fish and chips but one would never dare to eat them walking along the street. It was just not done, in Llandrindod.

Llandrindod was no mediaeval town with narrow lanes and twisting cobbled alley ways. Rather it was a sheepwalk and not a particularly attractive sheepwalk at that. This gave the town's early planners a clean sheet to start with unimpeded by ancient buildings or the ruins of an historic castle. Of this, they took full advantage and designed broad streets, spacious squares and road junctions. They dammed the outflow from a marshy hollow and created a fine boating lake. They designed bowling greens, a golf course and tennis courts, realizing that physical

41

exercise was as least as necessary to their overfed clientele as their disagreeable waters. These welled out in a pretty dingle where grew some noble trees. This they turned into a public retreat and called it Rock Park. Here they installed a Pump House where they sold the life-giving waters at a penny a glass.

Skirting the town flowed the River Ithon, a rather sluggish stream and hardly characteristic of Wales, but abounding with trout. Thus the sport of fishing was added to the attractions of the town, with the mud-loving carp in the lake for the fishermen who love just to sit and con-template.

Today, only the faithful few come to imbibe the waters but the town offers other attractions: the beautiful valley of the Wye is not far away and the lonely Radnor Forest is equally near with the Roman Fort of Castell Collen only half a mile away.

BUILTH WELLS

Builth has the history that Llandrindod lacks. Llewellyn the last Prin-ce of Wales sought sanctuary here when fleeing from the English. It was refused by the lord of the castle and the prince was turned away. In spite of turning his horseshoes round to deceive his pursuers, he was caught up with at Cilmery a few miles away and slain. A great pillar of stone beside the main road marks the spot today. Good patriotic Welshmen may attribute the disaster that befell the town in 1691 to the treachery of its inhabitants in refusing sanctuary to Prince Llewellyn. A great fire destroyed the whole town as the judgement of the Almighty, they say. The town, as we see it today, therefore, dates only from the rebuilding af-ter the fire and looks old but not ancient.

The grand old bridge over the Wye dates similarly to the 17th cen-tury. Hopelessly inadequate for modern traffic, it was widened some years ago. In the cycling days of my youth, I used to look over the parapet of this fine old bridge into the river below. It was a rare occasion when I did not see two or three fine salmon, their heads facing upstream and their fins and tails gently waving to keep them in the current. Whether from poaching or change of habit, I never see them today.

The Wye is a canoeist's dream and the stream inits gorge from Builth to Glasbury, a canoeist's paradise. Every hazard from rapid to cataract faces him as he makes the exciting passage. This should be made in gym vests on a warm summer's day and only by swimmers, as cap-sizing is an accepted risk and the whirlpools are deep.

Those who know the limpid stream of the Wye only in summer have no conception of the vast billow of yellow water that fills the arches of Builth bridge when the melting snows of the Cambrian Mountains send down their floods. Drowned sheep and sometimes cattle are borne

42

along or stranded on sandbanks, along with the trunks of trees the river has gouged from its banks. The Wye has beauty in Summer but Fury in Winter.

The water-swallowing rites of Llandrindod affected Builth in less degree. The town had its pump room and the Old Crown Hotel aped the fashion of Beau Nash in Bath but the craze never really caught on.

Today, it is the Welsh farming community that has put Builth Wells on the map. Each year, farmers from every corner of Wales flock to Llanelwed across the bridge for the Royal Welsh Agricultural Show which takes place on a permanent showground. But Builth is the mecca of farmers only one week in the year; it is the rendezvous of the lovers of Nature's beauty the whole year round.

CHAPTER SIXTEEN

ABERAERON. DREAMTOWN OF AN ENTERPRISING WELSHMAN

Visitors to the pleasant seaside resort of Aberaeron will notice at once that here we have no Mediaeval township with narrow streets and tortuous alleys, but a town built on modern lines with broad streets and dignified buildings. This town, that might have been planned by a Roman Proconsul is the dream town of a Welsh squire who had inherited wealth. It needed a horse and sledge, (Wheeled carts were not common in his day), to carry the treasure from Monachty to Tyglin.

The enterprising squire who dreamed up a seaport was the Rev. Alban Thomas Jones Gwynne who, unlike some of his breed, did not squander his wealth and the rents of his tenants in riotous living.

In those days, (the beginning of the nineteenth century), there was no good seaport between Cardigan and Aberystwyth to bring lime to the farmers' fields or culm for their fires. But there was the river Aeron which could be deepened to carry sailing ships and a fertile valley that could grow crops for export.

The first thing Gwynne had to do was to build a breakwater to control the tide and keep his new harbour from silting up. A clever mason named William Green from Aberystwyth was employed to do this and afterwards to build the quay where the ships could unload. Good stonemasons flocked to the work from all over the county and soon the quays were built and the river dreged. Ships began to arrive at the new seaport and warehouses rose to store the trade goods. The town began to grow. It was not long before ships began to be built in the new harbour and David Jones and William Harries brought their shipbuilding skills from Aberarth to bustling Aberaeron. They were traditional shipwrights with inherited skills in building ships from family experience in building fishing craft. With no book knowledge or slide-rule calculations, they could build a ship from keel to truck perfect in every detail building first a scale model. The local woods were searched for the oak to build the ships, especially timber shaped naturally in the growth of the tree to fit the contours of the hull.

As trade began to boom, skilled artisans in every branch of building construction flocked to the town and every ship on the stocks had its blacksmith for the necessary iron forgings. Notable among the blacksmiths was Thomas y go, (Thomas the blacksmith), who set up his forge a hundred yards up the river which drove his great hammer, Y myrth wl Mawr capable of delivering a blow each second.

This is now preserved in the National Museum of Wales at St.

Fagans but the water wheel that drove it is still where it was installed. Thomas y gof was a great blacksmith who forged edge-tools for all the farmers around, but his masterpiece was the famous Welsh Shovel, the heart-shaped, crank-handled shovel with which all Welshmen dig their gardens. It was noted throughout Wales from the slate quarries of Llanberis to the mines and docksides of Glamorgan. Its virtues were its long-wearing qualities due to the imprint of the Great Hammer on the steel.

There was no bridge over the Aeron river in the early days of the port. The road through the town passed along the eastern side and it was here that the river was bridged. Workmen in the shipyards at the harbour had to cross the river by ferryboat, an original type of ferryboat that ran on cables strung across the harbour. It was a sort of box suspended above the water and was wound across the river by a pully. The fare was a halfpenny. The remains of the cable anchorage can be seen today on the grassy bank across the river.

While the skilled jobs of the port were done by specialist artisans, the unskilled labouring work was done by a colony of Irishmen housed on the beach in rough quarters called Bedlam Barracks. These workmen had their own school for their children, provided at the expense of Gwynne near the ruins of an ancient fortress known as Caer Cadwgan. Cadwgan Square opposite Pwll Cam is named after it. An exceptionally high tide finally swept away these ruins and invaded the school. The children had to be rescued by boats.

In building his dream-town, Gwynne exacted the highest standards in design and appearance. The great architect Nash is said to have been at his elbow. Only the finest Victorian architecture was permitted in the building of houses, hotels and business premises. One has only to look at the streets surrounding Alban Square to notice the overall plan. The end buildings dominate in size and dignity of appearance. The Town Hall itself has a nobility rarely seen in a small town and Portland House has an air of majesty to compenstate for its plainness of architecture.

The Feathers Hotel has Victorian dignity but its spaciousness did not match up to modern requirements. Its front portion was built by a local squire, Major Lewes of Llanaeron, but it is said that Gwynne himself was obliged to finish it.

The standard of design for house building was not so exacting. Masons Row is functional. It housed the colony of masons as Vulcan Place housed the shipwrights. Ships' captains who chose houses overlooking the harbour showed their pride in their ships by naming the houses to which they retired after their ships. Thus we have Aeron Belle overlooking the harbour and Aeron Maid and Aeron Lass are also to be found. The house Aeron Queen carries the ship's name to this day.

Thus Aberaeron, once a village of poor fishermen, became a bustling, thriving seaport with 70 sailing ships going down its slipways in the years of its growth and heyday. But the days of the sailing ship were numbered with the advent of the steamship. The proud sailing ship, battling against the westerly winds of the Severn Sea would take a week or more to round the point of Milford Haven on its voyage from Bristol. Often it was obliged to shelter in the Haven itself as storms made the passage perilous when threading the island ways. The steamship forged her way regardless of wind and tide. Thus, to maintain her trade, Aberaeron abandoned the proud schooner, the lordly brigantine and the lowly ketch and turned to steam. The tradesmen banded together and had their own steamship built on the Clyde. To the ringing of church bells and the hooting of sirens she sailed into Aberaeron harbour to announce a new era in coastwise and foreign shipping. Vainly the sailing ship, driven at low cost by the wind, struggled to keep her trade against the more reliable newcomer, but it was a losing battle. Road material from Penmaenmawr, pots and pans from Bristol and oranges from the Canaries came more speedily and more regularly. But soon, the steamship itself was doomed. In 1911 the railway came to Aberaeron with its quick door-to-door deliveries cutting the cost of transport and ousting the steamship. The sad tale of progress continues today. With better roads, the ubiquitous motor lorry has killed the railway and both sailing ship and steamship are no more than history along the coasts of Wales. The fine harbour of Aberaeron now floats a new breed of sailing vessels: the dinghies and pleasure boats of the holiday-maker. Offers of weekly or monthly cargoes are made from time to time by shallow draught shippers but Aberaeron is not interested. The Summer bonanza of the seaside holiday maker has replaced the trading enterprise of both steam and motor ship, but what a wealth of interest to the holiday maker if a little coaster tied up at the quay where once the three-master lay. The holiday-maker is king in Aberaeron today. He fills the hotels and guesthouses and crowds the shops. Warehouses that once sold coal now sell ice cream and honey and holiday gifts are the stock-in-trade of the shops. But Oh for the masts and pennants of ketch and schooner and the smell of pitch and tar!

CHAPTER SEVENTEEN

SHANI BOB MAN

Everybody round New Quay knew Shani, (Jane). They called her Shani bob man, (Shani, all over the place) Nobody knew where she hailed from but some said she was of gipsy origin. She lived in a tiny two-roomed shack on the beach at Cei Bach, propably abandoned by some fisherman of the days when herrings swarmed in the bay. Those were the days when sailing ships were built at Cei bach and lime was burned on the beach. Shani's shack has long since been claimed by the sea and only a portion of the lime kiln remains.

Shani lived in her shack by Squatter's Right, supporting herself on parish relief of three shillings a week and by selling eggs from her hens. Her nannygoat gave her milk and she travelled round the district begging what she could not afford to buy. Mr. Jack Davies of Gilfachreda tells how, as a schoolboy, he used to call on Shani with a friend to run errands for her for a ha'penny. 'She would come to the door, he said, 'wearing an old trilby hat tied down with a red and yellow handkerchef knotted under her chin'. She wore an old check shawl over her shoulders, clogs on her feet and the broken stem of an old clay pipe in her mouth. Her face was lined and weatherbeaten and her expression dour and forbidding. It was better not to cross her. Sometimes a spring tide would invade the floor of her shack. 'Davy Jones has been with me in the night', she would say as she sent us off along the beach to collect driftwood. When we had collected a big enough pile to please her, she would sit us down and give us a couple of boiled eggs to eat in our hands. For herself, she would often collect cockles and prawns boil them them and make a meal of them when boiled.

Often she was out of tobacco and she would say 'Go up to Griff Jones and ask for a fill of tobacco'. If we returned empty-handed she would say, 'Be off with you' and turn her billygoat on us. He was a fearsome creature and we ran for our lives but she would soon blow a whistle and call him back.

Shani had a sharp tongue for those who tried to pull her leg. Mr. W.D. Jones, a retired schoolmaster told me that his father used to farm Llwynon Farm and Shani would often call to cadge a fill of tobacco. For fun he would sometimes say he was out of tobacco. But Shani knew he was teasing and rounded on him, drawing attention to his unshaven face, 'Going about looking like an old gorse bush', she'd say. Mrs Jones, the farmer's wife baked once a week and Shani knew the day. She turned up as the bread was coming from the oven and there was always a loaf for her. There was also a dinner for her at the farm table at Christmas but on

New Year's day she was not so welcome.

A First Footer has to be a dark person to bring luck and should always be a man. Shani failed to qualify under either head.

Welsh miners holiday making at New Quay would hire a boat to take them to Cei Bach to visit Shani. She welcomed them and would put on an act calling her hens and goats by name and when they came for titbits making out they knew their names. Before the visitors left Shani's box would come out from under the bed ready for the coppers.

When no visitors were expected she went her rounds calling at farm and cottage, and, with doggerel poetry she sang the praises of the generous and lambasted the stingy. One would give her a loaf, another a lump of cheese, a third a cut of bacon. Rarely was she empty-handed.

She also sold her hen and duck eggs to visitors and Mrs. Evans of Gilfachreda was a regular customer. 'How do your hens always lay such lovely brown eggs?' asked Mrs. Evans on one occasion.

'I'll tell you if you promise not to tell anybody else', replied Shani, 'I just stain them with cold tea.'

Mrs Evans wrote a book, (in Welsh) about New Quay in which she said that Shani regularly attended the local Methodist chapel and was a trenchant critic of the sermons preached. If the sermon did not please her, she would call it 'Cawl dwr', (Watery soup). In chapel she preferrd to sit 'in the bodies', (where they placed the bier at funerals). 'You dont have to pay a seat rent there', she said.

One morning, Captain Thomas, who lived above Cae Bach looked out of his window and said. 'There's no smoke coming out of Shani's chimney this morning. I'll go down and see if she's alright'. Pushing open the door of her shack, he found Shani lying on the bed fully clothed. Shani was dead. Calling the police, he looked over the cottage and dragged out a big heavy chest that stood in the corner. It was locked. They fumbled for the key in Shani's pockets, found it and opened the lid. To their amazement, a great hoard of coppers, sixpences and threepenny bits met their gaze. A horse and cart was fetched, the chest was loaded on it and taken to the bank at Aberaeron. The money was counted, about £120 and at the bottom of the chest was Shani's will. She had left it all to Aberaeron Cottage Hospital. Shani had lived on charity but her heart was in the right place. Her savings were meant for charity.

CHAPTER EIGHTEEN

HISTORIC VILLAGE

The village of Llanarth bestrides the main road from Aberaeron to Cardigan where the little river Lleithi runs at the bottom of a picturesque gorge and, where an old mill called Pandy used to weave woollen cloth from the wool of the local sheep. In the Middle Ages and, indeed up to the last century, the village centre was not in the gorge but at the top of the cliff that forms one side of the gorge. There, round the ancient church the houses clustered. The church is a Celtic foundation but when the Normans came, they built the massive tower and changed the dedication to one of their own saints.

Linking the newer village in the gorge with the old village on top of the hill near the church is a steep road called Rhiw Vylltyg. Beneath a cliff along this road, legend says that the Devil rested. He was carrying one of the bells from the church to take to his cronies at Llanbadarn Fawr and although the spot is only a short distance from the church it is said that the curch bells cannot be heard from there to this day.

The church itself carries many legends of which the most well-known concerns the antics of the Devil. His favourite hideout was on the north side of the church where he would lie in wait till an infant was brought into the church to be bapitzed. He would then enter through a doorway, (Now blocked up), and attempt to claim the infant as his own before baptism had secured it for Christ. The ancient font, now kept just inside the church door bears out this legend as it carries four prowling lions at its base to protect the infant from the attentions of the Devil. Another legend speaks of other activities of the Devil. He would enter the belfry when a baptismal service was being held and create a racket to drown the parson's voice. This went on till the exasperated parson took bell, book and candle and entered the tower to exorcise him. As the parson mounted the stairs the Devil retreated before him till he reached the top of the tower. Unable to retreat further, the Devil threw himself from the top of the tower to the ground. Unfortunately for him, he landed on a sacred stonecross which, (also inside the church door,) still carries the hollows made by his knees and elbows.

A few years ago the oldest inhabitant of the village, Evan Lewis Evans, lived with his daughter Bessie near Pandy, the old woollen mill. He was 92 when he died after spending most of his working life as estate carpenter to the Longcroft gentry of Llanina. 'Years ago' said Evan, 'there was no public water supply in the main road village, if you wanted pure drinking water, you had to climb Rhiw Vylltyg with a bucket and fetch it from Fynnon Gloch, a spring near the church.

'In those days', he went on, 'the post office was up there and the postmaster was a sort of unofficial dentist; he removed teeth at sixpence a time, much cheaper than the doctor. 'The village fairs were held up there too, in a field behind the church, still called Cae Fair. There were all kinds of goods on sale, including beer which was sold from the barrel. There were plenty of drunks on Fair Day. If incapable, the policeman carted them off to the Pound and left them there to sober up. (Parts of the wall of the pound are still to be seen). 'The village was self-contained in those days with two tailors, three shoemakers, three bakers and a village shop that sold everything from groceries to flannel petticoats and bootlaces'.

I knew also another old resident who lived at Pencae. He was Evan Jones who in his younger days, worked for the council carting chippings brought by the ships to Aberaeron.

'The main road was narrow in those days', he told me. 'A deep bog bordered it and part of his work was to cart rough stones the farmers had collected from their fields and dump them by the side of the road to make a foundation. Stones from the local quarry were also dumped in heaps and old men, (and old women too) sat on stools with hammers breaking them up for sixpence a day'.

He remembered too the first solid tyre motor lorry that tried to make the journey to Cardigan. 'It slid into the ditch half-way up the hill', he said and had to be pulled back on to the road by a team of horses'.

Another old resident who lived up by the church was Captain Varney. He was an old man, but even in age his weather beaten features carried the determination and challenge of authority. His seamanship was learned in the little sailing ships that sailed from Aberaeron and New Quay and by the age of 27 he was in command of his own vessel. His proudest moment was when he was in command of S.S. Jersey City, a steamship of 10,000 tons. 'A lovely ship' he told me.' He 'I brought her into Hartlepool harbour with timber piled on the deck as high as a house'. He was an old seaman who died in his bed. Gravestones in Llanarth churchyard tell of others 'Lost at sea', for the village, in common with New Quay has been the nursery of sailing men.

CHAPTER NINETEEN

TWM SHON CATTI. THE WILD WAG OF WALES

Long ago, in the little town of Tregaron, was born, a notable character named Twm shon catti. Tradition says that he was the illegitimate son of Catherine Jones of Tregaron by Sir John Wynn, Lord of Gwydir. He was born in poverty of a widowed mother and, at nineteen, after trying one or two peasant occupations, he became a clever thief. His genius for deceit enabled him to alter the appearance of animals he had stolen so that he was able to sell them back to the very persons he had stolen them from. One day, he encountered a robber along the road. Mounted on a sorry nag, Twm was carrying a bag of money of small value on an errand for a farmer. The robber, on a fine horse, with a brace of pistols in his holster, demanded the money but Twm refused to hand it over. A struggle ensued during which Twm threw the bag over the hedge and told the robber to go and get it. While the robber was scrambling through the hedge, Twm jumped on his good horse and rode off leaving his own nag behind.

Twm's rogueries were legendary but some of the stories told about him are regarded by some historians as pure fictions. What is less well known is his fame as a bard and herald. He made himself knowledgeable about the pedigrees of all the gentry of the country, and, as Welshmen are proud of their ancestry, all the notable people commissioned him to trace their pedigrees. He was well paid for this and would trace a client's pedigree right back to the ancient princes. In this work, Twm was not always scrupulous over dates and details, but he had to please his wealthy clients and small errors were overlooked. It may be that some of his pedigrees were, in part, forgeries, which probably accounts for a Pardon that was granted him under the Great Seal in 1559, forgiving and cautioning him.

For his thieving and irregular conduct, the officers of the law were often on his track to apprehend him and bring him to justice. This drove him, at one time to live in a cave on the road to Ystrad Ffin. The cave is to be seen today on top of a rocky hill above the gorge of the Tywi at Ystrad Ffin. It is not the usual sort of cave but a hollow place beneath an enormous slab of rock accessible only through a narrow aperture and by a person bent double. When 'in residence', Twm kept a sword handy to be ready to decapitate an intruder who could enter only in a crouched posture. Today, visitors make their way in hundreds to the cave, recording their visits by carving their names on the rock inside.

When I visited, some years ago, there were countless names scratched on the rock some with dates going back before the last century. The

51

place is wild and remote and reaching it involves a bit of scrambling up slippery slabs but the path is well marked and many find it.

Twm chose a cave in this district in order to be near his ladylove, the heiress of Ystrad Ffin. Knowing Twm's reputation, her father had banned him from the house and locked his daughter up in an outside room with a barred window. But the love was mutual and Twm would come by night and hold converse with the lady through the bars of the window. He begged her to marry him but her father had forbidden talk of marriage and she would not agree. Finally, on the orders of her father, she refused to see him any more. Twm pleaded and she agreed 'Just once more'.

'Give me your hand in parting', said Twm, 'and I will say Goodbye'. She extended her hand through the bars and Twm took it in his. Having grasped it, he took his sword and said, 'Unless you promise faithfully to marry me, I will cut off your hand.' According to historian Meyrick. Twm arranged for a priest to be at hand when he was holding the lady's hand through the window. On her agreeing to marry him, he produced the ring and with the blessing of the priest, slipped it on her finger.

There is no need to consider whether Twm would have carried out his threat. He knew the lady loved him and would marry him when no longer prevented by her father. For his part, Twm was content to wait. When eventually the father died, the wedding took place and, together with his new wife, Twm found himself the owner of the Ystrad Ffin estate with land and property in his own right.

As lord of Ystrad Ffin he became a changed man, dropped his freebooting habits and became the model of respectability. It was not long before he was appointed to the office of High Sheriff, previously held by his father in law. The one-time thief and rogue was called upon to sit in judgement on thieves and rogues. From personal experience, he knew the ways of the fraternity and how to deal with them. It is said that while he was High Sheriff of Carmarthenshire, a man could travel through his domains with a purse of gold in his bosom and go unmolested.

CHAPTER TWENTY

THE LEGEND OF PONT EINON

Pont Einon is the bridge that spans the Teifi river as it emerges from Tregaron Bog. Nearby is the ancient farmhouse of Penybont, home of Cardiganshire gentry in the past and today of one of the most substantial farmers in the county. The farmhouse kitchen is so vast and the fireplace so capacious that in times past they used a pony to drag in logs for the fire.

The legend concerns the owner of Penybont before a bridge was built across the river. He was a man named Einon, who, before he inherited the farm was engaged to be married to the heiress of Penybont. As the time drew near to their wedding day, Einon unaccountably disappeared leaving no clue to his whereabouts. Time passed and as he did not return, he was given up for lost.

In due course, another suitor to the hand of the heiress was accepted by the lady and the date of the wedding was fixed. The night before the wedding a great feast was held at Penybont with singing and playing on the harp. That same night a ragged wanderer called at Maesglas on the other side of the Teifi asking for a horse to enable him to cross the river which was in flood. The Maesglas farmer refused until the wanderer whispered in his ear and disclosed his identity. The horse was produced and stranger and farmer crossed the river and entered Penybont while the festivities were at their height. The farmer told the wanderer to remain in the kitchen while he entered the festal chamber. He stayed to hear the new bridegroom sing and play on the harp; then he announced to the wondering company, 'There is a man in the kitchen who can sing and play far better than this man'. The wanderer was brought in and asked to demonstrate his prowess on the harp. As he sang and touched the strings of the harp, the heiress began to weep and her bridegroom to be turned on the stranger saying, 'You are making her weep and tomorrow we are to be married', Begone wanderer! 'On this, the singer drew aside his cloak and shouted, 'Myfi bia'm ty, am telyn, a'm tan. Ios a rhywun, ti aiff allan.'

The lady rushed to his arms and the new suitor was sent packing. It was Einon, back from his wanderings. His promised bride had recognized him and the wedding did take place after all. When it was over, Einon said, 'I will never again risk the Teifi in flood. I will build a bridge'. The bridge was built and stands today, sound, solid and noble but too narrow for modern traffic. Beside it the County have built a new wide bridge of concrete but the old bridge remains, a proud monument to bridge building two hundred years ago.

MIGRATION OF THE SHEEP

When April's chilly prelude to summer warmth is past and the cold mountain winds give place to kindlier airs, the 'marginal' farmer beneath the stark moorlands of the plateau begin to make preparations for the annual migration of the sheep.

We had a marginal farm in a valley below the mountains of Tregaron and we longed for the day when our sheep would be banished from the lowland pastures to 'Summer it out' on the mountain. They were hardy Welsh Mountain sheep, able to forage and find subsistence on the coarse grasses of the mountain as soon as the tough molinia began to put forth the tender shoots of Spring. For weeks since the snows of winter had disappeared, the sheep had been the chief headache of the farm, breaking fences and invading the fields of young grass we were reserving for 'Early bite' for the cattle. The bold leader of the flock, in spite of sticks tied crossways to its head would find the weak spot in the fence and break through to the forbidden territory of the next field. The rest of the flock, knowing the routine, would stand waiting patiently till the rogue ewe had found the way through and with happy bleatings of anticipation would follow her in the long line of invasion.

By this time, the spring lambs had arrived and our neighbour, Tommy Brynhownant, had snipped their ears to mark them with the earmark of our farm. The weaker ewes had been selected to remain behind for a little longer.

Soon came the day for the spring trek to the mountain gate, beyond which they would spend the Summer. To the accompaniment of bleatings of anxious ewes, for the moment separated from their lambs and the treble cries of the lambs that had lost their mothers, the trek would begin. Shepherd Mike was in charge with his dogs, Fan and Gwen, leading his flock from behind (like the Duke of Plazo Toro), whistling the dogs to head off deserters that tried to head back to the farm.

After a couple of miles, the mountain gate was reached, a rickety affair tied up with baling wire. (When it's everybody's business to repair it, it's nobody's business). There were several farmers in the valley who had rights of summer grazing on the mountain and those rights were recorded and the areas marked on a map in the vicarage as the parson used to levy tithe on all farm lands.

Once through the mountain gate, Mike drove his flock upwards to our traditional grazing ground.

It was near the edge of the escarpment overlooking the deep valley of the Brenig, a dry area where the young spring grasses appeared first. Old fences delineated our grazing area but long since the posts had rotted and the wire had rusted. The sheep could wander far and wide but the older ewes knew their stamping ground and the flock was never far from their traditional grazings. These mountain grazings were 'Crown Lands' orginally claimed and thus designated in the reign of Queen Elizabeth I and inviolate ever since except where some squatter from the valley below had established his Tai Unos and settled. These Tai Unos, (Houses built in one night), were a mark of the poverty of farming in the last century. A young man, with no land of his own, would select a likely area of Crown land and, with the help of friends build a hut of turves to live in. Tradition said it had to be done in one night and if smoke was coming from the chimney by daylight, he was the owner of the land around it as far as he could throw an axe from the door. There was no Tai Unos on our bit of mountain but further up the valley there had been one in living memory. Old residents remembered it and the lady who lived there. She used to go down to Tregaron shopping and would say to friends she knew, 'I must be getting back to Buckinum Palace' when it was time for her to go home.

Our sheep never strayed far from their appointed area on the mountain and we did not disturb them till shearing time. When this time came, Mike would go up to look at the washing pool in a stream in the next valley. Was the dam intact? Were the stone walls which guided the sheep to the pool unbroken? Perhaps some repairs were needed. These done Mike called his dogs, collected the sheep, and drove them to the pool and made them swim to the other bank. This was to wash their wool as unwashed fleeces fetched a lower price than washed. Having been washed, the sheep had to be shorn the next day but that's a separate story.

After shearing, the sheep were taken back to the mountain. This time there were no stragglers. It was June and the mountain grasses were at their best. There is good feed in the young shoots; the ewes thrive and have plenty of milk for their lambs. The lambs grow and, as they are weaned, they are brought down and fattened for sale on fields of rape.

When the chill winds of late October announce the onset of another winter, Mike would bring the whole flock down to the lower pastures. The cycle in the life of a mountain sheep was once more complete.

SHEARING DAY

Shearing Day, like threshing day and potato planting was communal event in our valley under the Tregaron mountains. The valley farmers were a community and each farm contributed its labour force to help its neighbours complete the job in a day. Tommy Williams of Brynhownant, the biggest farm, was the undisputed organizer of farm shearing days so that these did not clash. It was he who determined the day on which we sheared our sheep. These had been gathered and washed the day before and brought under cover in the farm buildings so that their fleeces would not get wet if it rained. The barn had also been cleared and the floor swept the day before, the shearing benches put out and a big wool sack hung up to take the fleeces.

About 9-30 the following day the shearers would begin to arrive clad in their overalls and each carrying his newly-sharpened shears wrapped in cloth. After the inevitable cup of tea, they all sat down at their benches waiting for the sheep to be brought to them by the catchers from the pen adjoining. The catcher placed the sheep on its back in front of the shearer who proceeded to tie three of its legs with a cord to prevent kicking. This done, the shearer began to shear the wool, starting with the belly and working round to the sides and back, keeping the fleece intact, all in one piece. As each sheep was shorn, a helper gathered and rolled up the fleece in a tidy roll and placed it in the sack. Very little was said as the work proceeded; each shearer concentrated on his task for Welsh shearing men are jealous of their skills with the shears. No blood must appear on the sheep's flesh from clumsy handling of the shears but the pot of Stockholm Tar was handy to anoint any accidental nick. The only spoken words were the cry of 'cordie' telling the helper who handed out the ties to bring one at the double. The cry of 'Down carrier' was also heard as each shearer finished a sheep and wanted it taken away so that he could start another. The 'Down carrier' took the shorn sheep and laid it on the grass outside for any signs of footrot to be cut away and for any cuts to be treated. All this done, another helper untied the sheep's legs first marking the sheep with the farm's distinctive mark.

As the shearing proceeded, the farm women and their daughters began to arrive to help in the kitchen. No rough farm garments on this occasion ; instead, pretty frocks and polished shoes and a pinafore for the cooking jobs. The sale of the wool was one of the chief items of the farm revenue and a good wool clip added to the prestige of both farm and far-mer. Shearing was also a social occasion. Friends were invited from the village for friendly gossip.

With all this help from neighbours, the dinner preparations were taken out of the hands of my wife Dora, but she was not content to sit and watch. Her Welsh friends could peel potatoes and cook the meat but she wanted to express her English individuality. The usual 'afters' on the neighbours' farms were rice pudding and jelly. Dora's ideas ran to fruit pies and custard so she made this her part in the proceedings.

The men were called in to dinner at twelve. The fully extended table groaned with enormous dishes of vegetables and the men helped them-selves. Welsh custom decrees that no woman shall join the men at the shearing dinner table: the woman's job is to prepare and serve the din-ner. When the men have eaten, the women's turn will come.

Everyone ate in silence. The main job was eating and talk hindered eating. When the last person to clear his plate was ready, the men rose and returned to the barn to smoke and talk till it was time to continue shearing. Towards three o'clock one of the ladies came over to the barn to see whether shearing was nearly finished and to see if it was time to prepare tea.

The afternoon shearing was more relaxed as the number of unshorn sheep dwindled. With only a couple of sheep to go there was competition as to who would be left with the last sheep. He would have to finish it alone.

Then the call to tea. If dinner was eaten in silence, everyone talked over tea. The work was done and tongues were loosed. Conversation was lively but all in Welsh and beyond our comprehension. After several loud guffaws, I ventured to ask Tommy Pantsheriff to translate the joke. 'Oh', he replied, 'It's all about Mr. X and somebody else's wife'. There were more leg-pulls of a similar nature, often bawdy, usually indelicate or with a Rabelaisian flavour. The Welsh are no prudes.

Tea over, someone mentions feeding stock and milking cows and with thanks from the hosts our neighbours depart to their farms, reminding each other that the next shearing will be at Dan Jones, Penpompren or perhaps with Richard Lewis of Bronwydd.

Thus were we grateful to our Welsh neighbours as the techniques of operations such as shearing were beyond us.

THE BLIZZARD

Christmas morning dawned with that horrible East wind sweeping down our valley, funnelled from the bleak wastes of the mountain moorlands at its head. As we drank our morning tea the weather prospects were bad but not terrifying: just another cold wintry day. Snow began to fall lightly after breakfast, but it was Christmas Day, and we must go to church on Christmas Day. Mike started the ancient Armstrong and we went to church in comfort. The snowflakes were falling thickly when we came out, the wind had increased; and as we went back up the lane, drifting had begun.

Back at home we began to attend to the more vulnerable of the stock: the cows. These had left their ration of kale and were sheltering under a hedge. Mike fetched in the cows to their stalls in the 'beudy' while I went to look at the hens down by the river, taking with me a bale of straw to make their house comfortable. Hens are perfect nit-wits. They were sitting under the bushes with the snow gathering about them. Foolishly, I assumed they would return to the shelter of the house on their own so I left them. To make sure I returned later to find them still cowering under the bushes in the driving snow. I had to chase and catch them one by one as they flapped helplessly in the snow. They did not have the sense to seek the shelter of the house on their own.

With the cattle and the poultry now safe, Mike and I went to look at the sheep. The Welsh mountain ewe is a hardy creature but we had to make sure. We climbed the Bank where they were grazing, taking the dogs with us. Up on the exposed Bank the wind was teriffic; we could not stand upright and the dogs were blown off their feet. Crawling on all fours, we had to close our eyes to narrow slits as the snow, fine as dust, bombarded our eyeballs. We could see no more than a few yards but there were no sheep. Sheep have the instinct of self preservation so we looked for them in the wood below. There they were, sheltering among the trees, so we left them and returned to the shelter of the farmhouse. We had done what we could.

Dora managed to produce the usual excellent Christmas dinner, after which we had the customary distribution of Christmas parcels and sat down round the fire in preparation for the next ordeal at feeding time.

Meanwhile the blizzard was reaching its height with the snow drifting and filling the lane.

After tea, Mike milked the cows and I saw to the hens; then we turned in for the night, wondering what the morning would bring.

It was a white world we saw but the gale had blown itself out and we could see the sun. The problem now was how to get our milk to Tregaron in time for the milk lorry. Near the house the lane was full of snow but we could see clear patches beyond so we went to work with shovels, clearing the lane as far as the milk stand where the milk lorry usually came. Here we met Tommy Brynhownant, Dan Penpomren and Alun with their churns of milk. We were now a team but the lane was hopelessly blocked from here onwards. The only possible way was to cross fields and get to the top road. Luckily the wind had blown the snow off the fields into the hedges and gateways so it was only necessary to clear the gateways. This we did and our tractors with their loads of churns were at last on a road that was fairly clear. Just outside Tregaron was the biggest drift of all but we went to work on it with our shovels and cut a way through. Reaching Tregaron square our hopes of the milk lorry were dashed; it had been unable to get through.

What to do? There was the train and someone said it was running. It passed Pont Llanio where the milk factory was, so to the station with our churns. The railway had saved the situation.

We had struck one of the hazards of farming in Wales: the hazard of winter snow. For the first time we realized why the mountain farmers, at the onset of winter, stocked up with sacks of flour and piles of groceries. In heavy snow they were isolated from Tregaron and the shops by miles of snowdrifts. We were only hindered. Their sheep, too, had no wood to shelter in, their only shelter were the hollows and cwms with the snow piling on top of them. No wonder the mountain farmers lost 80 or 90 per cent of their flocks in the terrible winter of 1947.

CHAPTER TWENTYONE

KING OF THE MOUNTAINS

On the lonely road that leads from Tregaron to Abergwesyn, where the drovers of the last century used to drive bunches of cattle across the mountains on their way to England there is a farm called Pantsheriff. It was the last farm in the valley to cut and burn peat. The smell, so pleasantly pungent, of burning peat in Tommy Pantsheriff's fireplace is in my nostrils now, so many years afterwards.

In the mid-1700's, Pantsheriff was the home of Sheriff William Williams, High Sheriff of Cardiganshire and self-styled 'Brenin y mynydd', (King of the mountains). He was a man of supreme intelligence, iron resolve and autocratic demeanour: a man to be feared. His sheep pastures were vast and he counted his flocks by tens of thousands. A greedy man, he was always quarrelling with his neighbours and filching bits of additional land where he could. He would allow a poor peasant to 'squat' on his mountain for a shilling a year rent then, as the tenant improved the land, he would raise the rent until the man could no longer afford to pay. He would then give the tenant notice to quit and claim the improved land as his own. If a lawsuit followed, he called as witness a notorious liar named James Ffrwd and invariably won his case. Even today an accomplished liar is called James Ffrwd by some of the older people.

Once Williams fell out with James Ffrwd and chose another witness. James Ffrwd thereupon threatened to appear in court for the opposing party. Williams gave in. 'Go to Tregaron fair', he said to his servant, 'and buy a good horse and take it to James Ffrwd'. The bribe was effective. James Ffrwd changed sides again.

Sheep steeling was a hanging offence in those days. 'Never be tempted to steal my sheep', he warned his tenants. 'The hangman's rope is waiting'. Even his shepherds he distrusted. He would enter their cottages without warning and lift the lid of their cooking pots on the fire; he was always on the look out for evidence he could produce in court against a tenant. His tenant at Dolgoch was a bachelor who had a good-looking housekeeper to look after him. Williams was suspicious that they shared the same bed. He had no moral scruples about this but considered that unchastity was bad for early rising at lambing time. One day he visited the cottage and complained that he felt cold. While the woman was out at the peat stack to replenish the fire, he took the fire tongs and hid them in the man's bed.

Returning, some days later, he asked for the fire tongs to stir the fire. 'They seem to have got lost', the woman said. 'Go and look in the other bed', said the sheriff, as he took his leave.

The legend that survives with the greatest persistence among the mountain folk tells how the sheriff's boastful pride rebounded. He boasted to everyone that no one in the land owned more sheep than he. To prick his bubble of self-importance, a farmer whom he had bested in the courts spread the story that a lady in Scotland owned 20,000 sheep; 1000 more than the sheriff. When the story reached the sheriff's ears he was livid with rage. He drove his shepherds to distraction to increase his flock. The following winter was disastrous. The mountain sheep died in their thousands in the snow. In Scotland the winter was less severe; the Scottish lady escaped with fewer losses. The blow to the sheriff's pride made him more morose and intolerant than ever. He became a soured recluse, feared and hated by all the mountain folk.

One day a message reached him that his shepherd at Moel Prisgau was seriously ill and needed a doctor at once. The unwritten law of the mountains compelled immediate action; even the embittered sheriff could not ignore it. He sent a servant post-haste to Lampeter to summon the doctor. In his haste, the servant forgot to shut the mountain gate, a heinous offence in the eyes of the sheriff. Madly fuming, he got on his fastest pony but he did not overtake his servant till he was in sight of the tower of Lampeter church. Flaying the servant with vituperation, he ordered him to return at once to shut the gate on pain of instant dismissal. Then he could return for the doctor.

Another of his victims was a poor old widow who lived at Nant Stalwen. She was a fortune teller and he had wronged her in a dispute over sheep. He didn't ask her to tell him his fortune but she told it to her neighbours. The sheriff had a few Welsh Black cows grazing in the valley at Nant Stalwen and the widow's crystal ball told her that one day one of his black cows would have a white calf. When that happened, she said, the sheriff would die in that year.

Her prophecy came true. The white calf was born and the sheriff died soon afterwards. They buried him, unwept and unsung in the churchyard at Llandewi Brefi. The famous Welsh preacher, Daniel Rowland, conducted the service and chose for his text, the psalmist's words: 'I see that all things come to an end but thy commandment is exceeding broad'.

CHAPTER TWENTYTWO

SAFARI TO BRIANNE

The mighty Brianne reservoir is in the southern half of Mid-Wales but from the scenic point of view, it might be in Switzerland. A round trip to visit it can be made clockwise from Tregaron or anti-clockwise from, say, Llandovery. The choice is yours. It is equally beautiful either way, but I will describe it clockwise.

Starting from the ancient town of Tregaron, the first leg of the trip is to climb the mountains by the old Drovers' road along which the drovers of the last century took their bunches of cattle, ponies, sheep or pigs across the mountains to the markets of England. For the stony journey, they shod the cattle with iron plates on their hoofs in a field behind the Talbot Hotel in Tregaron and even made the geese walk through a mixture of tar and sand to harden their feet.

The road climbs the mountains up the deep valley of the Brenig stream, past the peat hags where, in less affluent days, Tregaron folk cut the peat they used for winter fuel. Reaching the top of the pass, the road descends to the valley of the Camddwr, crosses the river and runs down the valley beside the stream. This is the land of the Red Kite, a bird of prey almost extinct but today duly preserved. You may see a pair soaring above the valley, their keen eyes searching the bracken or heather below for signs of the little mountain shrew or lizard on which they feed. They can easily be distinguished by their forked tails or, on nearer view, by the russet plumage of their under feathers.

After four or five miles, partly hidden by a clump of trees, the little mountain chapel of Soar y Mynydd appears. Sunday by Sunday, the mountain sheep farmers of days gone by came here (on pony back) to worship leaving their ponies in the tiny stable at the end of the building. At the other end in those days there was a little school for the children of the mountain farmers and a schoolhouse for the teacher who conducted the school. The school has long since been closed as the highland farms have mostly been abandoned, their owners drifting to kindlier lands in the valley. No regular services are held in the chapel today, except in the summer when visitors form the congregation and a preacher from a lowland chapel arrives to take the service.

Just below the chapel, one of the arms of the great reservoir begins and your road leaves the valley to climb the hill to the left and cross a mountain divide that separates this arm of the reservoir from the greater arm over the mountain ridge.

Reaching the summit of this dividing ridge, a little road goes off R. to a mountain farm that has been abandoned. It was called Nant Neuadd and I remember it when it had a sound roof and the walls were intact. Damsons grew in the garden and its former occupants, Tommy and Lottie Williams were continuing to look after their sheep that grazed the mountains around.

From the summit of the 'bwlch', the road descends to the Tywi arm of the reservoir which it crosses by a concrete bridge. Just before the bridge it passes another old sheep farm, also abandoned but still with its walls and roof intact. This is Bron yr helm, once one of the chief farms of the mountains with upwards of 3,000 sheep, but now taken over by the Forestry Commission for growing trees.

Across the bridge you strike a very ancient road that once ran down the valley, but is now submerged beneath the Tywi arm of the reservoir. In its place, the reservoir builders have provided a fine tarmac road that rides high above the magnificent lake, now looking down upon its waters, now winding in and out of cwms and valleys to follow its contours.

Now the trees begin, for this has long been Forestry Commission territory: young trees: spruce, larch and pine clothe the steep slopes of the lake margins in a garment of green. In a couple of miles, a road strikes off up a valley towards Abergwesyn and the sheep grazings in the Irfon valley. The farm that owned the sheep now lies beneath the waters of the reservoir. It was a thriving farm till the great snows of 1947. Hardly a fraction of the sheep were alive after this disastrous winter and the farm was abandoned. It was called Fanod as was the gorge beside it where the river flowed. It was a frightful gorge with the river at the bottom of a rocky slit a hundred feet drop and so narrow at the top that the farmers called it 'The cocks' stride'. An active man could have leapt it.

While the reservoir was filling, the farm ruins stood stark and gaunt overlooking the rising waters till eventually even the chimney was beneath the flood. A glorious country, this land of Brianne: a land of deep forested cwms, of craggy, heather-clad rocks, of winding road revealing at every bend a new vista, a new scene of delight. The road winds in and out of little side valleys, each with its tiny stream; its little contribution to the great reservoir. And down below, seen through the trees or revealed in its wide expanse from some pomontory, lies the reservoir itself, half-filling the gorge and growing in width as it nears the dam. One side arm runs into the mountains and the road must go round it, circumnavigating each of its tributary valleys along an upper contour. Finally, after a detour of a mile or more, it returns to the main valley with a panoramic vista of the union of the two main reservoir arms and the forested mountains beyond.

In another mile the reservoir lies hidden behind a mountain buttress till the road to the dam appears; a road carved out of the solid rock of the mountain side to provide stone for the dam. A rocky ledge leads to the car park overloking the dam. This is a massive structure of rock with a core of clay to prevent seepage. From here are views both up the two miles of the main reservoir and also up its side tributary the Brianne that gave its name to the whole reservoir.

From the car park, you look down the deep steep-sided gorge spanned by the dam. It carries the overflow from the reservoir and becomes the river Tywi. The reservoir supplies the city of Swansea with a constant supply of drinking water and cools the steel of Margam.

Your tour of the reservoir ends at the dam but the spectacle of gorge and river continues with the undammed river Doethie contributing its volume to the now-attenuated Tywi making it once more the major river of South-west Wales. The junction of Tywi and Doethie is most impressive. One looks down upon it from the high crag above the confluence with a side road leading to it; a wonderland of rock and wooded gorge.

CHAPTER TWENTYTHREE

THE ANCIENT CHURCH OF LLANWENOG

Of all the works of man, ancient churches tell the story of the past the more eloquently. Castles fall to enemies and only ruins remain to speak to us but churches are preserved by their very sanctity. Of these, the church of Llanwenog is a notable example. It was founded in the thirteenth century by a female saint called Gwenog, a woman so virtuous that she rejected all male blandishments and became a nun.

The date when she built her church is buried in the mists of antiquity but tradition says that the sight she first chose was rejected by God: what was built by day was demolished during the night. The saint therefore became interested. She directed a muscular mason to take a heavy hammer and throw it in a southerly direction. By divine intervention, it landed in the spot God had ordained for the church to be built. The work then proceeded without interruption. God's direction of the proceedings was perhaps prompted by the existence of a spring of clear water bubbling out of the earth just below the present churchyard. This would quench the thirst of the masons as they worked. This blessed spring became later a place of pilgrimage that cured children suffering from spinal weakness if they were immersed in its waters before sunrise. It has since dried up, whether or not from modern irreligion we dont know.

Built at last with mud and water the church stood for three centuries as a Celtic foundation, probably with a Celtic bell-cote. In the fifteenth century, Sir Rhys ap Thomas became its patron. He it was who with the valour of his Welsh subjects on Bosworth field, placed the Welshman Henry VII on the throne of England. This powerful prince, as a memorial to the victory of Bosworth, replaced the Celtic bell-cote by the great square Norman tower we see today. He did not neglect either to add his signature to the work in a stone bearing his arms over the window in the tower on the west side.

ROMISH SYMBOL

An interesting story attaches to the Holy Water stoup built into the interior masonry at the base of the tower. It was slung out at the Dissoultion when Henry VIII destroyed the monasteries and forgotten. In later years it found its way to a blacksmith's shop. The blacksmith filled it with unholy water and used it for cooling his red hot irons. An antiquarian lady discovered it and, knowing it to be historic, had it built into the wall of the tower.

ANCIENT FONT

In the side chapel is an old rood screen and an ancient font. Dating from the days when the Devil was a real live personality. He had to be deterred from snatching the souls of babies brought to be baptized. For this purpose the font was carved with grotesque faces which were intended to put him off.

The Belgian Refugee

The most significant feature of the church interior is the beautiful carving of the pew ends. These pay tribute to the skill of a Belgian refugee in World War I. He was Joseph Reubens, a wood carver by profession. Driven from home when the Germans occupied Belgium he used his talents in wood carving to the glory of God.

AN IRISH ROBBER

In the Middle Ages Irish adventurers swarmed to Wales, some with peaceful intentions as George Owen relates: to brew whisky and sell it round the farms: others came to steal and rob. One of these was Carn Philip Wyddyl, the leader of a gang of thieves that haunted Llanwenog. When pursued by the local Welshmen, this worthy entered the church, claiming holy sanctuary. The Welshmen pursuing him did not consider him as worthy of the protection of the church and chased him up the tower. From the top, he jumped to the ground, only to be captured by those waiting below. He was stoned to death and buried under a cairn or mound of earth which still bears his name.

AN ANCIENT CUSTOM

In the rolicking, frolicking days of the Georges and the Victorians there were inter-parish competitions often of a boisterous nature. One of these was a game of ball played on foot or on horseback. It was an annual competition between the men of Llanwenog and the men of Llandysul. The ball was a well-greased wooden ball and the object of the game was to knock or carry the ball to the door of one of the competing churches. Heavy sticks or cudgels were used to direct the ball but it was all in the game to use them on the heads or bodies of the opposing team. The losing team had to buy drinks for the winners as each side nursed their broken heads in the pubs after the match. As no holds were barred, broken heads were plentiful but copious supplies of beer allayed all feelings of resentment and eased'the consciences of those who wielded the sticks. At Llandysul, some humanitarian spoil-sport replaced this interesting custom by a religious competition, much to the disgust of the would-be players.

CHAPTER TWENTYFOUR

HERO OF THE BALLOT BOX

In the beautiful valley of the Clettwr that surges down through picturesque wooded ravines to join the Teifi, lies the historic hamlet of Rhydowen, (Owen's ford). It is named after Owain Gwynedd who, in 1131 came down from the North with an army at his back bent on conquest. He crossed the ford but was met and beaten by the prince of South Wales after a bloody fight near Llandysul. A contest, not bloody, but no less momentous, was enacted in this village in the 1870's. It was a contest to decide whether the village squire or Parliament should govern the country. For centuries the landlord was paramount. His tenants and all beneath him were obliged to vote in elections as he wanted on pain of dismissal or eviction. Parliamentary Reform was in the air and Liberals demanded a secret ballot, but they had to fight long standing tradition. Their champion at Rhydowen was the minister of Llwynrhydowen chapel, the Unitarian chapel that stands on the crossroads. He was Gwilym Marles, an M.A. of Glasgow University, a man of high integrity and moral principles. He saw the injustice of the system that bound the souls and intelligence of servants and tenants to the will of the landlord and he fulminated from the pulpit against the squire of Allt y rodyn who was landlord of the whole district.

The squire, John Davies Lloyd, was of ancient stock. His forebear, one Kadifor, had won fame by capturing Cardigan Castle from the Normans by scaling the walls with his men. For this exploit, his prince, the Lord Rhys, had rewarded him with vast lands, the hand of his daughter in marriage and the right to mount three scaling ladders on his escutcheon. His descendants had held Allt yr odyn from time immemorial.

Although a drunkard and a gambler, Lloyd was inclined to be paternalistic towards his tenants, but when his reckless extravagance threatened to ruin his estate he appointed a solicitor's clerk named Allen to take charge of his finances. Allen was a different kettle of fish; he was ruthless with tenants who voted the wrong way and evicted them without mercy. Finally he persuaded Lloyd his employer to close the chapel from which Gwilym Marles preached. In law, he was entitled to do this as Lloyd was ground landlord of the place. Thus the chapel door was locked leaving Marles and his congregation without a place to worship. The owner of the local woollen mill lent them a room in the mill but, in due course, Unitarians from all over Britain subscribed to build them a new chapel. Meanwhile, Lloyd's evil genius, Allen continued to manage the estate and the landlord went from bad to worse in his dissolute behaviour.

The unfortunate man had lost his father when he was two, removing all restraint in his upbringing. Before he came of age he was living with a ballet dancer and he boasted to his friends that he drank whisky before breakfast and champagne afterwards. Finally drink sapped both his physical and mental powers and he complained that he could no longer put out a candle with his duelling pistol; his hand shook so much. He did not come of a family of wasters. His grandfather had been a distinguished member of society: a barrister, high sheriff, M.P. and a generous benefactor to the parish with a plaque to his honour in the church of Llandysul.

Gwilym Marles and his congregation struggled on in make shift rooms while his new chapel was being subscribed for and built while the evicted tenants sought employment as labourers or emigrated to America. The fate of one family was tragic. During the voyage to America, three of the children contracted smallpox due to the insanitary conditions on the emigrant ship. They died on landing. Broken in means and spirit, the father and mother returned to Wales where the mother died of a broken heart and, hopelessly in debt, the father soon followed her to the grave.

John Davies Lloyd died at the age of 28 in 1878 leaving the bulk of his estate to Allen. The will was considered so unjust to his wife and family that there were many appeals and the case went from court to court. Finally Allen was granted £5000 and the rest of his estate went to his wife and to his sister, to be held for her children. The inhabitants of Llandysul had followed the case with interest and great were the rejoicings when Lloyd's sister, a Mrs. Massey arrived to take up her inheritance. A carpet was laid from the carriage of her train to the carriage that was to take her to Alltyrodin. But the crowd would not let her go with such a welcome, Brawny arms took the horses out of the carriage and siezed the shafts. To the music of the Tregroes Drum and fife band, they drew the carriage through the streets with the whole town out and cheering as they went. Outside the town the horses were put in again and off they went to llwynrhydowen where Mrs. Massey alighted and threw open the gates and door of the chapel to the waiting congregation. Gwilym Marles was not there to take possession. He was probably too ill as he died the following year, worn out with trouble and worry. He lived just long enough to see the new chapel they had built for him but not to be its minister. He had fought the good fight, he had founded the Llandysul Grammar School and his name was revered by everyone. His old chapel is now a museum of Unitarian archives.

CHAPTER TWENTYFIVE

AN ANCIENT CHURCH AND A FIERCE BATTLE

Only a mile or two from Cardigan stands the ancient church of Mwnt, (Mount), beneath the pointed hill from which it takes its name. The church dates from 1380 or thereabouts and was built about the same time as St. David's college at the cathedral. But whereas the latter has been in ruins for 300 years, Mwnt church still stands four square to the elements with only minor alterations. It has an ancient granite font capacious enough to immerse the whole body of the infant as was done in ancient times.

Until the year 1853 the nave held five pews belonging to and occupied by the five principal families of the parish. The remainder of the congregation had to provide their own seats or stools while the very poor used to sit on stone seats against the walls of the nave. Originally there were two entrance doors: the parson's door and the people's door, but about 160 years ago, with the birth of democracy, a Mr. David Evans closed up the parson's door leaving only the people's door.

The roof is held up by seven massive couples of old Welsh oak, secured, not by nails, but by wooden pins.

In olden times a rood loft separated chancel from nave but when this disentergrated from age, it was taken down and the remains of the carved worm-eaten timbers placed in public view. Beside these old timber fragments is a descriptive account of the history of the church. It tells how pilgrims of old rested here while waiting for favourable weather for their sea passage to Bardsey. They prayed in the church for calm seas.

The cosy little cove below the Mount with its lovely sand and cliff walks in both directions has always tempted visitors, and, at one time, a local owner of the land was proposing to fence off the field above and make a charge for visiting. Fortunately, just in time, the National Trust stepped in, took over the whole area and assumed control. Thus, this delightful historic spot was saved for the nation. The National Trust indeed make a modest charge for their control is praiseworthy.

In olden times the natural shelter of the little cove enabled the little sailing ships to come in and discharge their cargoes of limestone and coal. These were burned together in the kiln that stands high up on the beach to produce lime for the farmers' fields.

In 1155, the shelter of the landing place tempted a force of Normans and Flemings to attack the native Welsh from behind. They were seen approaching round the point of Cardigan Island and the warning beacon on the mount was lighted. The Welsh forces gathered and were ready for the invaders when they landed. Leaving their boats, the attackers had to climb the steep sandy slope at the head of the cove and, as they struggled to the top, the Welshmen descended on them with the flashing swords and blood-curdling cries. The battle was fierce and bloody but the Flemings were at a disadvantage, they had to fight uphill exposed to not only the swords of the defenders but to the flights of their arrows. The Normans and Flemings were slaughtered to a man and few got back to the boats in retreat.

When the battle was over, the victors buried the bodies of the vanquished in the sand with their own dead. To this day, when strong winds disturb the sands, human bones, it is said, come occasionally to light. It was a Mediaeval 'D' Day and today it is still remembered as Sul Coch, (Bloody Sunday).

Thus the peaceful field where visitors now park their cars was once a scene of carnage and the little rivulet that descends to the cove ran red with blood.

CHAPTER TWENTYSIX

A GOOD LANDLORD COMES TO A BAD END

The old mansion of Dolaucothi, since raised to the ground, was once the home of John Johnes, a talented and influential man: a magistrate, a County Court Judge and an enthusiastic geologist. Opposite his home were the Roman gold mines of Pumsaint, then being worked. He would reward the miners who brought to him the Roman gold ornaments they found in the old workings, the necklaces and bangles intended for wives and sweethearts back home in Rome. He made a collection of these which he sent to the British Museum.

In his youth, like most of the old landlords of Wales, he was a hard drinker, a 'three-bottle' man, they called him; but whisky did not spoil his aim with the shotgun. For a bet, he once shot twenty-seven out of twenty-eight swallows as they flew beneath Pumsaint Bridge. His memory went back to the early years of the nineteenth century when, so he told his tenants, there were scarcely any wheeled waggons or carts in the neighbourhood; the farmers used sledges. When waggons and carts came to be used, the roads were so bad that it took three or four horses to pull them. This he said in defence of the toll gates and the tolls the farmers complained of. 'Today, with improved roads', he reminded them, 'two horses can pull a cart that once needed four'.

It is not generally known today that the gold mines were in operation only thirty years ago. On our farms at Tregaron we once employed a man to dig a well who had worked in the Pumsaint gold mines. He used to talk about breaking into ancient Roman workings and finding tools left behind by the Romans. He was a strict Mehtodist and refused point blank to join in a sweep on the Derby.

Alongside his County duties as Magistrate and Judge, John Johnes was an efficient agriculturalist. He saw to it that his fields were properly limed and cultivated and that his properties were well kept and maintained. His tenants respected him and during the Rebecca Riots when angry farmers destroyed toll gates, no gate was destroyed on his property.

The learned and intellectual atmosphere of Dolaucothi attracted eminent men in Art and science who found a warm welcome under its roof and everyone was happy when tragedy struck. Johnes had a butler named Tremble who had been with him for seventeen years; an Irishman with a quick temper. When the tenancy of the local Dolaucothi Arms became vacant, Tremble wished to become landlord and asked his employer Johnes to back his application. Whether Johnes was reluctant to lose Trembles's services as butler or whether he considered him to be

71

unsuitable as landlord we dont know, but he refused.

Making a final appeal to his employer but with murderous intent, Tremble entered the room where Johnes was sitting, taking with him a loaded shotgun. Johnes again turned down his appeal so Tremble raised the shotgun and fired both barrels into his master's stomach. He then rushed into the next room intending to kill Johnes's sister but was prevented by the cook who stood in front of her. She received a charge in the leg, from which she was for ever afterwards lame.

The murderer afterwards shot himself and they buried him in the churchyard at Caio. But the villagers of Caio would not have him; they dug him up and carried the body to Tirabad in the next county. The Tirabad people would not have him either. They returned the body to Caio where, after much deliberation the Caio people buried him again outside the churchyard wall.

CHAPTER TWENTYSEVEN

A HISTORIC CHURCH

In the dim mists of the Dark Ages, say around the year A.D.500, a saint named Tysul founded the church of Llandysul. Today, the town's name enshrines that of the saint.

Christianity, at that time, was a tender plant struggling to establish itself in a land of pagan worship. St.Tysul was one of its apostles.

We dont know whether St.Tysul built his wattle and daub church where the present church stands today as there are signs that show that it might have been on Pencoed foel, the hill that overlooks the town. The chief indication lies in the ancient altar now built into the altar of the Lady Chapel. This ancient altar was found on the slopes of Pencoedfoel.

By the time the Romans had left Britain, the gentry of that day were still using the Latin language and adopting Latinized names. This is evident from an ancient inscribed stone built into the wall of the choir vestry. This stone formed part of a stile leading to the churchyard and, when found, it was incorporated into the church wall. Its inscription commemorates a certain pious lady named Velvoria and tells us that she was the daughter of a Romano-British chief called Brohomaglus. Other carved stones, taken from the church wall were built into the altar of the Lady Chapel. One of these has a carving of the Crucifiction with Christ hanging on the cross and the Virgin Mary and St.John, one on either side.

Moving on a few centuries to the days of Edward I, the mud and wattle church of the Dark Ages had, under the Normans, been replaced by a building of stone with a low tower. Even in those days the church had importance as it was valued by Pope Nicholas IV at £20, a lot of money in those days. This money was supposed to help defray King Edward's Crusade expenses but it probably went towards paying for his wars in Wales.

From the Middle Ages, historical time jumps two centuries to the days when Puritanism was in the air and the Roman Catholic religion was being challenged. Bishop Barlow of St. Davids jumped on the Puritan band wagon, derided images and the bones of saints and enriched himself on religious grounds by stripping the lead from the roof of the lovely Bishop's palace. He would have done the same with the cathedral itself but for his master Henry VIII. 'No; not where the bones of my grandfather lie'. Henry's religion was tinctured by greed and self enrichment.

It is no doubt true that religious credulousness among the pilgrims had diverted great wealth to the coffers of St. Davids and that monks and abbots had grown fat on the simplicity and gullibility of the masses but there was no piety in Henry's rape of the monasteries. Perhaps it was as a counter gesture that the canons of St.Davids cathedral were granted the revenues of Llandysul church, among others.

In the days of 'Popery' the church had a rood loft, a piscina and a lepers squint. All that remains today of the rood loft are the stone steps by which the priest reached it. The piscina is missing although a stone vessel in the choir vestry might have served. Maybe Cromwell and his Reformation vandals were responsible for the loss of the original piscina. The lepers' squint, however, is to be seen today, screened by the organ.

The 13th century tower of the church has been raised four times from its original twenty feet to its present seventy-three feet as indicated by the stones in its construction. These can be traced to the bed of the Teifi and three local quarries, but the date of the grand stone pillars and arches is probably the date when the side aisles where added to the nave. At the time of these alterations to the body of the church, the roof was raised. The line of the original roof can be plainly seen in the distrubance of the end walls supporting it. The date when the side walls of the nave were replaced by the masonry pillars and arches is not known but it was probably done when the roof was raised. The original walls were whitewashed.

It is quite possible that all these alterations with the addition of the side aisles were done at the grand restoration of 1874. The comparative newness of the masonery gives substance to this supposition. The cost of the whole work was £2,300, a considerable sum in those days.

The bells in the tower were hung in 1777. Their timber framework became so worm-eaten and delapidated that a short while ago the present vicar, the Rev. I.D.John was obliged to have them re-hung with new timber. This, with the massive job of repointing the walls of the tower and the reconditioning of the organ cost the church upwards of £12,000 which, even now, has not been fully repaid.

In the old days, the church had wealthy patrons in the local gentry. Today the cost of its maintenance rests upon the townspeople and it is to their great credit that this noble structure bears today such a cared-for appearance.

CALAN HEN

The memorial lych gate of the church was erected in 1933 to commemorate the replacement of a barbarous custom with a religious observance. The barbarous custom was the playing of a black wooden ball in a sort of Victorian hockey match between the stalwarts of Llandysul and the heroes of Llanwenog. This followed a sumptuous, gargantuan repast given by the farmers to their men in recognition to loyal service in

74

the harvest field. This was accompanied by generous libations of beer so that by Kick-off, every man was either wholly or partially drunk. I have described elsewhere this boisterous game in which the object was to knock the ball against the door of the opposing church. Heads were broken and blood flowed in the contest in which animal barbarity took the place of rules in the game.

In 1833, the vicar of Llandysul decided that this annual blood-bath should be replaced by a contest more in keeping with the religious role of the church. With the cooperation of all the churches within eight miles of the town, he established a competition in answering catechisms, singing anthems and reciting the scriptures to take the place of the ball game. The festival of Calan Hen has taken this form ever since.

The lych gate stands today as a memorial to the piety and humanitarian instincts of the Rev. Enoch James who changed the form of the festival in 1833.

CHAPTER TWENTYEIGHT

A TOWN THAT MINDS ITS OWN BUSINESS

'My face is my fortune, Sir, she said'

Thus Llandysul, whose setting with the Teifi at its foot bears the charm of a Swiss 'Thal'. Its houses rise in terraces, their gardens kissed by the mid-day sun. The other side of the valley is a wooded 'allt' that completes the Swiss illusion. In the valley bottom, the Teifi surges and crashes among rocks and boulders, a perfect venue for canoeists who come from all over Britain to measure their skills against its riotous waves and eddies.

The town has a religious rather than a warlike history. No Norman baron made it his stronghold but devout pilgrims to St. Davids or Llanddewi Brefi often passed through in the Middle Ages. One of these was St. Tyssul who founded the mud and wattle church before the Normans gave it its square tower. The local inhabitants of those ancient times may have been peaceful enough but their princes were not. The fair lands of the Teifi valley were held by a prince of South Wales but were coveted by Owain Gwynedd the prince of North Wales. Their armies met on Pencoedfoel where the South Walians dug entrenchments, (still to be seen). Chroniclers say it was a bloody engagement but, blood letting was a mere pastime in those days.

The infamous Vortigern, dissolute king of the Britons, tried to hold out against the Saxons on Craig Gwyrtheyrn just up the valley but his fort was burned down and he fled to Anglesey where 'for his sins', (according to the monks), a thunderbolt from heaven put an end to his wicked life.

Another stronghold of an ancient prince was Castell Gwynionedd, half a mile from the town. You can reach its moated defences only by scrambling on hands and knees up a precipitous slope.

Fights tended to be wordy rather than bloody in the 18th century. The supporters of John Wiles, (The cloth cap brigade), foregathered in the Wilkes Head while the stalwarts of the landlords assembled at the Kings Arms. Fierce riots broke out in London and heads were broken but the battles in Llandysul were of the tongue.

Although the population of the town in the mid 1800's was not much above 500 there were over 20 pubs. These were much more than beer houses in those days. They were centres of learning where people of education kept schools. They were also centres of social activities and each had its Club or savings society.

There was no mayor and corporation but the office of mayor was filled by a self-educated townsman named Evan Isaac. To him everyone went with their troubles and disputes; he was father-confessor to the whole town. He was secretary and treasurer to the Porth Club that held its meetings in the Porth Hotel, meetings that were conducted with the dignity and decorum of a borough council. No mayor with chain of office could have commanded more respect and deference than Evan Isaac.

Evan was no bigot but he had had a rigid puritan upbringing and he frowned on boys playing marbles or cricket on week days, let along Sundays, and yet he would cheerfully mend their bats in his workshop. He had the Puritan horror of images and pictures of sacred people in places of worship and yet he enjoyed decorating the church at Easter and Christmas. Although he did not drink himself, he had no objection to those who did, in moderation and he would enjoy helping the landlord of the Kings Arms to tap a barrel of beer. To his family he was something of a martinet and his children feared his reprimands although they were not afraid of him personally. As a craftsman in wood he was superb. He would walk miles to find a suitable tree for a special job and when he had found it, he would borrow a cart and take it to the sawmill at Pontwelly to have it sawn to his liking and properly seasoned. He was a friend of Gwilym Marles the Unitarian minister of Llwynrhydowen chapel and relative of Dylan Thomas. For him, he made sets of wickets for the boys.

Although the railway had, by this time, reached Llandysul, goods still came by sea to Llangrangog, the nearest seaport. Sam Morris, the son of Ebenezer Morris who was a brother in law to the famous Henry Richard was a sea trader in oak bark and a tanner. The ship he built at Llangrannog was called the Anne Catherine with a cargo-carrying capacity of 324 tons. Her cargo was copper and guano which tells us that this little wooden sailing ship made voyages as far as Peru.

Llandysul had its lock-up for lawbreakers in those days. It was at Tymaen and the story is told of a Mr. Thomas of Dol-llan who was confined there on bread and water for some offence. Knowing his propensities, his servant Twmi took beer to him in a jug. He could not, of course, get this into the cell so he got a rubber tube and supplied beer through the bars.

CHAPTER TWENTYNINE

BRECON AND THE BEACONS

Brecon started its mediaeval carrer as a Norman town complete with castle to hold back the turbulent Welsh who lived in the wild mountains to the North. When the mood was on them these fierce natives would come down from their hills to raid the fat lands of the Usk valley and drive home the herds of prime beef. The Norman Bernard of Newmarch was the castellan whose job it was to keep them back, helped by the Norman Picard whose stronghold was Tretower. More peaceful times came with the Tudors who put an end to all this fun and games and persuaded Norman and Celt to beat their swords into ploughshares and live in peace. So, from being an embattled town, Brecon turned to trade an the monks of the Benedictine Priory no longer feared the fierce Welshmen. The Priory, in later years, became the cathedral but that was not until 1923 when the Diocese of Swansea and Brecon was formed. The remains of the old Priory are still to be seen with great thick walls like a fortress but its fine Norman font and its thirteenth century choir now grace the resotred Cathedral. And beautifully restored it is with all the dignity of a cathedral.

If Bernard de neufmarche' was the first Norman to lay violent hands on the rich vale of Usk, his sins were pardonable compared with those of De Braose who succeeded him. This orgre, according to Gerald de Barri, invoked the sanction of the Almighty to find justice in his cruelties and treachery. He invited all the local Welsh princes to a banquet in his castle at Abergavenny, 'provided they left their arms outside as a matter of courtesy'. When the wine was flowing and the feasting was at its height, he gave the signal for his own armed men to burst in and slaughter the lot. He then went down on his knees and thanked God for His cooperation in the enterprise.

Gerald de Barri seems to have been fond of bringing a touch of humour into his writings as when he talked about the beavers in the Teifi river. These animals, according to Gerald, were hunted, not only for their skins but for their private parts which the natives considered a delicacy. Having already been robbed of these essentials, says Gerald, the intelligent beaver, when pursued by the dogs, would cock up a leg to show that they were missing.

Again quoting Gerald, it seems that the church of St. David, at Llanfaes across the river bridge, had miraculous powers in guarding its sanctity. A boy who had chased a pigeon into this sacred place was punished by his hand sticking to a stone and not coming free until he had knelt down in repentance. This miracle was repeated with the mistress of a

78

church dignitary who was no better than she should be. She had sat down on the stone and found herself stuck with her clothing and also part of her anatomy on which she sat. It required many prayers of repentance before she was freed.

Charles I, as a fugitive after Naseby, sought santuary in the Priory of St. John, but the style of his welcome is not recorded. It could hardly have matched the loyalty he received at Raglan castle where the aged castellan, a Herbert, opened his treasure chest in a vain effort to repair the kings' fortunes. No money was offered at Brecon, only hospitality and the solace of mediatation. But, at least, Brecon escaped the Roundheads.

For whatever reason, they sent Napoleon's captured officers to Brecon but their incarceration was not very severe. They were allowed a daily promenade along the bank of the Usk, but whether they were permitted to do more than ogle the Welsh girls is not recorded. The riverside where they exercised is still known as 'The Captains' Walk'.

Coming nearer to today the great actress Sarah Siddons while performing at Brecon, stayed at the Shoulder of Mutton inn in the High Street with her brother, Charles Kemble.

The great landmark, the Brecon Beacons, looks benignly down on Brecon and the lovely valley of the Usk. As the highest mountains in South Wales, they afford a magnetic attraction to climbers both from the comparative ease of their ascent and from the wonderful views of their summits. The tarn, only 700 feet below thier topmost crags is legendary like Llyn fan fach, the lake that nestles in the hollow below the Carmarthen Van. This was the lake of the fairy bride of the local farmer whose sons became the clever physicians of Myddfai. The tarn beneath the summit of the Beacons is said once to have had an enchanted island only accessible by a tunnel from the shore. The island rose out of the waters only on May Day when fairy flowers could be gathered there to the sound of fairy music. These flowers were so lovely that a sacriligious visitor brought some away with him and carried them down the mountain. When they faded, the island disappeared below the waters and has never since been seen.

Since 1949, the whole area of the Beacons and Fforest Fawr has been a National Park and, in 1961 a Mountain Centre was established on the moors near Libanus.

Tourists flock here all through the summer to enjoy the freedom of the hills, the charm of the open moorland and the peace and relaxation offered free of charge at this unique resort.

For water sprites, there is the Brecon Canal; 25 miles of glorious waterway that was made at the time of the Industrial Revolution to carry coal and iron ore to Brecon and the furances of Brynmawr and Blaenafon. Today, its derelict locks have been restored and it is a holiday haunt for canoeists and power boat fans, with the river Usk as its constant neighbour.

Still a market centre for cattle and sheep with a fine museum for the antiquary, Brecon also offers salmon and trout fishing for the angling votary and many country walks for the energetic.

LLANGORSE

Sitting in a shallow depression in the hills to the east of Brecon is the largest natural lake in South Wales: the lake of Llangorse. Tradition says its waters are deep but its gently shelving shores give the opposite impression. Of all the lakes of Wales Llangorse abounds in fish, from pike of fabulous size to eels so long that there is a saying, 'Long as a Syfaddan eel'. From time immemorial fish have swarmed in this lake, a penernnial source of food for the lakeside dwellers. The ancients fished from canoes made from dugout tree trunks and in 1925 one of these was found stranded in shallow water the level of the lake was low. In primitive times, for safety from their ememies, familes lived in huts built on foundations of stakes above the waters of the lake itself, and hut circles have been identified on the surrounding hills.

In the reedy shallows in one part of the lake live flocks of ducks, geese, moorhens and other varieties of aquatic birds secure from disturbance by the evolutions of speed boats that tear about the surface on summer days.

Tradition says that once a 'faire citie' stood where the waters now roll and vivid imaginations see the traces of former buildings as they peer down into the depths. Tradition also says that an earthquake in prehistoric times swallowed up the 'faire citie.' The mediaeval orge De Braose leaves his unsavoury reputation in a farm called Tref Trahairn near the lake. He treacherously beheaded the young Trahairn as he rode to meet him.

VALLEYS OF CASCADES AND WATERFALLS.

The great plateau of Fforest Fawr that rubs shoulders with the Brecon Beacons is carved by deep gorges whose depths hold the grandest waterfalls in Wales. The gorges have been carved deep into the limestone plateau by two rivers, the Neath and its tributary the Mellte. The remote fastnesses of these spectacular gorges are off the beaten track and known only to the lucky few, for they are heralded by no teashops or ice cream stalls or crowded car parks. You can reach them from the Vale of Neath, (A 465), in the south or across the plateau from Senny Bridge, (A 40), in the north. The twin rivers, the Neath and the Mellte both hold waterfalls but the latter has the finest display. To reach it, you strike off the main A 465 at Pont Nedd fechan and take the mountain road to Ystrad-fellte, just past the Angel Hotel. After two miles the wide verges of the road give room for parking, and, on both sides there are notices: 'Take your litter home'. Here a cart track goes R and soon you reach a gate that is locked, with a stile beside it. The locked gate keeps out cars but the stile encourages walkers. A path avoids a derelict farmhouse and continues across a rough field beyond. At the end of the field you reach the lip of the gorge and the roar of a waterfall is in your ears. The path now rough and steep leads down into the gorge through the trees with handy branches to hold to ease your descent. At the bottom of the gorge runs the river in its strait jacket of rock beneath its canopy of foliage. Now the path follows the river, steep-sloping but passable and the roar of falling water is near at hand. It is the first of three 'scwds', (Waterfalls), in the space of about three quarters of a mile.

There is a breathtaking beauty about this necklace of cascades and waterfalls not found elsewhere, even in Wales. The gorge is a fairyglen of tumbling water and naked rock in a setting of lush greenery. Each fall has its own individual characteristics: in some the water drops over a precipice in one majestic leap; in others the fall is broken by a ledge of rock in mid career.

Beyond the uppermost fall there is a footbridge across the river from which you can follow the stream down along the opposite bank with new exciting views of the falls. This path leads to a tributary stream, the Hep-tse, with the most marvellous fall of them all. It is called Scwd yr Eira (The Snowy Waterfall). Here the water plunges unbroken over a ledge of rock into a deep pool below. Behind the fall a trackway is recessed into the rock from which you look down the gorge through a curtain of falling water. This trackway dates from packhorse days when even loaded animals with bulging packs could cross the river without harm or damage to their loads.

The way back is the way you have come but there is a short cut if the river is not too high. A line of stepping stones crosses the river to reach the other bank near where you reached the gorge from the road. The stones are uneven and the footing is, in places, precarious, but at low water it is possible. The only risk is wet feet, but friendly hands can help over the wider gaps.

Back at the road it is about $1^1/_2$ miles to the Youth Hostel where you look for a little road going R. This road is narrow but it takes you to where the river goes underground for a couple of hundred yards. There is a Forestry Commission car park here and below is the Cavern of the White Horse into which the river disappears. A footpath above ground follows the river as it flows through caves and fissures beneath. At the

81

end of its underground passage, it wells up to the surface in a deep cavern to flow into a wide pool which looks tempting to swimmers. There have been drowning tragedies here in the past so a notice warns you against entering the water.

Here you are near the village of Ystradfellte with its ancient church and its churchyard with the tallest yew trees I have ever seen.

On the occasions when I have visited this waterfall wonderland, the popularity of the Porth yr Ogof, (The caves), has far exceeded that of the waterfalls themselves. There is always a scattering of visitors scrambling about the gorges of the waterfalls but the caves attract people by the hundred. I can only attribute this to ease of access and the handy car park. The waterfalls demand a short walk; the caves none at all (The seat of a car is very seductive.) But, in spite of having to walk across knobbly stones and boulders, many take torches and explore the caves if the water is low. Some even find a way through the underground tunnels and come out from the deep black pool at the other end, although how they manage it is a mystery as the only exit I have seen is by way of deep dark caverns of water. There are no Charons of the Styx to assist. The road goes on across the plateau from Ystradfellte to Senny Bridge, passing on the way an enormous monolith ten feet high called Maen Llia. This in olden times, marked a trackway across the hills when the lower lands were densely forested. It may have also marked the burial place of some ancient prince of the Dark Ages.